Oxygenate

Inhale Grace…Exhale Faith
Just Breathe!

By Lisa Rodriguez

Copyright © 2014 Lisa Rodriguez
ISBN-13:978-1505698114
ISBN-10: 1505698111

Printed in the United States of America

All rights reserved. No part of this book may be reproduced or transmitted in any form or by any means, electronic or mechanical, including photocopying, recording, or by any information storage and retrieval system, without permission in writing from the author.

Cover design: Shannon Smikowski

Dedication

This book is dedicated to my wonderful family and friends, who have supported me these many months:

To my parents, Josef and Kitty Gungl…you always prayed I would write a book. Thank you for believing in me.

To Dan & Ceci, thank you for letting me share your stories, so that others can see how BIG God really is!

To Caleb, you are such an encourager! And Camellie for your amazing talent. Thank you for pushing me beyond what I thought I was capable of doing, and keeping me on track…and did I say for keeping me on track?

To Carlos Jr. for always helping out with ideas and for being my "repair man." Where would I be without you?

To Collin and Angela, our forever "side-kicks." Your creativity is amazing, and I appreciate your constant prayers and support, even in the late hours!

To my father, David Hilton. Thank you for revealing the Master's Plan for your life and allowing me to see that nothing is impossible with God.

To my spiritual daughter, Sarah Hepfner, for sacrificing nights of sleep to help me through my "stuck moments." And to my faithful brother in the LORD, Mike Omo, whose dedication and skills amaze me!

To my dear friend, Shannon Smikowski, for pushing through every obstacle with a warrior-like spirit…you are incredible! And to my special sister in the LORD, Patricia Stauffer, for offering your gifts to help with this project.

Also to my Pastors at Oak Creek Assembly of God, for your prayers, support, and encouragement given to our family and ministry these 23 years.

To my sisters, who are a part of "Real Women Real Life," "Stepping into Leadership," and "Go Getters." Thanks for making life and ministry so much fun!

Finally, to my heart—my husband, Carlos, who has stood by me with prayers and love for more than 34 years. Thank you, for making my life so beautiful!

Endorsements

"Lisa Rodriguez is a Spirit-filled prayer warrior who has spent many hours teaching and preaching the Word. She knows about all the obstacles the enemy puts in the path of every day believers, and how to stay on course, overcoming in spite of them! In her first book, she shares lessons she has learned along the way, how to build on your faith and live in grace!"

Pastor Jerry Brooks, Lead Pastor
Oak Creek Assembly of God

"I believe there is one word which best describes Lisa and her ministry: PASSION. In Oxygenate, she was able to take what comes naturally to her verbally and capture it in this book. This work is 'Lisa on paper' and you are about to be recharged!"

Pastor Mark McKinstry, Associate Pastor
Oak Creek Assembly of God

"I've known Lisa for many years, and I know she is a woman after GOD'S own heart. Lisa has a unique way of bringing personal life stories and humor to this book that will make you smile. It's a great book to use for personal devotions and allows you to write down your own thoughts after each chapter. I'm someone who loves to journal so this is a great added bonus for me!"

Linda Scalish
Assistant Director, "Real Women Real Life" Ministries
Leadership Development Coordinator,
"Stepping into Leadership"

"Oxygenate" - what a wonderful work. It just begs to be ingested by God's people. Chapter after chapter it is filled with life-giving, spiritual oxygen tied clearly to the Word of God. Lisa's life is one that inspires everyone around her and she has outdone herself in this book. God has gifted her in using the practicalities of everyday life to help others see the deeper truths of God's Word and work as they partner with Him in their lives."

Laurie Ganiere
Re-Source Ministries

"Lisa's writing reaches deep into your heart, where you live, and gives you easy to understand truths that you can apply to your life in Christ. From personal stories to Scriptural applications, her refreshing style helps you move from, 'Victory to Victory'."

Carol Christensen, Director
"Real Women Real Life" Ministries

Contents

Forward written by Pastor Shawn Follis

1. Oxygenate
2. Fences
3. The Groundskeeper
4. Uprooted
5. Voices from the Graveyard
6. Dr. G
7. What's Bugging You?
8. The Holding Tank
9. When God Speaks
10. If the Enemy is Under My Feet, Why Is He Way Up There?
11. When Life is Stuck in Pause
12. The Sweet Fragrance of God
13. Waves
14. The Book of Remembrance

Do You Know Him?

Foreword

Just breathe. It sounds so simple. But if you've ever been in a place where your breathing has been interrupted, it can be terrifying. Gasping and straining for air, only causes panic to set in, making the situation worse.

Because breathing is both voluntary and involuntary, in those panic moments, you need to relax and allow your body to regulate. It may seem difficult at times, but you just need to trust in the natural process.

In our fast paced, self-sufficient world, it is easy to find ourselves running so fast and pushing so hard that we literally feel out of breath. Too many are chasing an elusive prize keeping them in this vicious cycle. If you are one of those people, you need to know that the only way to breathe again is for you to slow things down and allow your physical and spiritual life to find a natural pace.

Just as our physical bodies need oxygen to sustain life, our spirits need a fresh wind to energize the inner man. Neglecting this part of our life will only leave us stressed from life's circumstances, exhausted from the struggle, and desperate for the spiritual breath to survive. If this seems like your life, it is time for you to begin to breathe again. Take a few moments to invest in yourself by letting the words and stories of Lisa be a breath of fresh air to your soul.

Many things could be said about Lisa Rodriguez. I have had the privilege to partner with her in ministry and to walk alongside her family as they have grown, both spiritually and physically.

Lisa is a great communicator and prayer warrior; and she has a heart to help the people around her move from a place of hurting to a place of healing.

Just as a nurse is able to set an oxygen tube in place and regulate the flow to the patient, Lisa uses her passion for God and people to weave together a steady flow of biblical truth, scripture, and personal testimonies. You will find among the pages to follow, the ability to see how the constant outpouring of God's Spirit in your life is meant to infuse you with energy and passion.

So allow this book to be a source, to help you to stop struggling and trying so hard to make things happen on your own. Read one page at a time, and just breathe.

Pastor Shawn Follis, Youth Pastor
Oak Creek Assembly of God

.

Chapter One

OX·Y·GEN·ATE

*To supply, treat, charge or enrich with oxygen
(Oxford Dictionary)*

Oxygen—no one can survive without it. Yet as great of a necessity it is, no one really thinks about it, unless perhaps their lungs are compromised. Breathing just comes naturally.

In the Bible, it clearly states, *"The time came when the Lord God formed a man's body from the dust of the ground and breathed into it the breath of life. And man became a living person" (Genesis 2:7 TLB)*. This scripture reveals man was not actually living until he received the breath of God. From that moment on, mankind was provided with the ability to inhale oxygen in order to stay alive.

Likewise, in the Spirit, our oxygen comes through the very breath of God which permeates our being the moment we accept His Son, Jesus Christ into our lives. It is from that point on that we learn to inhale the grace of God; not just for the BIG moments we have, but for everyday life. This too should be just as natural as the air we breathe.

This lesson came to me during the birth of our fifth grandchild. Our youngest daughter Angela, and her husband Collin, asked Carlos and me to be present for the birth of their baby girl. That day came one day before our 34th wedding anniversary. Another reminder of how good God has been to us.

As Angela settled into the birthing room, Collin sent a text to their good friend Brandi Davis, who worked at the Women's Pavilion. Brandi hoped she would be working when Angela went into labor. Within minutes, she came bouncing in, all bubbly and full of laughter. Instant peace spread through the atmosphere, dissipating the anxiety Collin and Angela felt. It was obvious God had timed this situation and provided a friend to guide them through this exciting but laborious adventure! As I watched Brandi, I became captivated by her knowledge and the confidence she displayed. God's presence was upon her as she glided with ease from one task to another.

Watching Brandi made me realize there are times in life when it is important to stop… take a breath…and inhale God's grace which surrounds us. If we are observant, we will see His unmerited favor step into the arena of mankind in the most unexpected places, in the most unexpected ways, becoming like a choreographed dance from heaven. It will surprisingly be poured out upon the competitive surfer who catches a perfect, rippling wave of the ocean, or a painter whose calculated stroke of the brush brings notoriety; or in this case, a nurse who flows in the calling of God, helping to bring precious babies into the world.

Whatever experiences or assignments we may have, and no matter how big or seemingly small they appear, God wants to breathe upon us—literally oxygenate every part of our lives.

Think of this: even when babies are in the womb, they need oxygen, although it is not received through their lungs. Instead, it is supplied through the mother's blood transported through the umbilical cord. In our spiritual lives, our oxygen is supplied through Jesus's blood which is transported to us through the cross of Calvary. God's Word declares salvation is found in no one else, *"for there is no other name under heaven given among men by which we must be saved" (Romans 4:12 NKJV)*. Some may try and argue this point, stating there are other paths that lead to God, but He *"…is not the author of confusion" (1 Corinthians 14:33 KJV)*. He makes things simple for us to understand. Compare the two and it is very clear: God provided only one unique and intricate way to receive oxygen for life in the womb, and He has provided only one unique and intricate way to receive oxygen for life in the spirit. Both are through the blood. You can't argue what is truth…it's just God's design.

And as wonderful as all of this is, I guarantee there is so much more! Babies were never meant to stay within the womb or be forever tied to the umbilical cord. Sooner or later they must leave the protective compartment and live life. When our granddaughter, Mercy Rae was finally born, the doctor whisked her up and out of the canal and then proceeded to spank her on the buttocks. I thought it was a very cruel way to be welcomed into this world. But her momentary pain was for a purpose. That pain caused her to gasp—to inhale her first breath.

God's magnificent blueprint for bringing life into this world helps me to understand why our Christian lives aren't always easy ones. Even Jesus warns us, *"I've told you this so that my peace will be with you. In the world you'll have trouble. But cheer up! I have overcome the world"* (*John 16:33 GW*).

When we first come to know Jesus, the sense of joy is so great we naively think we will never again have any problems. Life just seems so good, so perfect. But sooner or later we will get slapped by the reality that life brings. It is hurtful…sometimes discouraging…but it too has its purpose. God never intended us to be attached to the umbilical cord of salvation neatly tucked away in a comfy place, disconnected from the world. His plan goes much further than our beginning moments in Him and far beyond the walls of the church. He wants us to crave for more than just our initial salvation. He wants us to inhale His grace, and in essence exhale the faith that changes the world!

This is His idea of living a true spiritual life: inhale grace, exhale faith…just breathe!

It is because there is so much more of this incredible life awaiting us, that God will not allow us to stay in the confines of a spiritual womb. In order for us to experience His love in all its fullness, He will literally cut the cord… and teach us to breathe.

"Like newborn babies, you must crave pure spiritual milk so that you will grow into a full experience of salvation. Cry out for this nourishment…" (1Peter 2:2 NLT)

Think About It!

1. The Word of God clearly states, the only way to God is through His Son, Jesus. Have you or someone you met ever thought there were other ways to God? Was there any evidence other than just opinion to back that up?

2. Do you remember a time when God's unmerited favor stepped into your life in an unexpected way? Was it something that was seemingly a small thing to others, but HUGE to you?

3. Do you remember that initial surge of joy you experienced when you first accepted Christ? (commonly referred to as the "honeymoon period")

4. Do you recall the circumstances when life seemed to "slap you" out of that honeymoon period and teach you to inhale God's grace for that momentary trial?

Write About It!

Chapter Two

Fences

Merriam-Webster Dictionary defines a fence as, "A structure like a wall built outdoors usually of wood or metal that separates two areas or prevents people or animals from entering or leaving."

It was a beautiful day and I was excited! Being only 8 years old, I was infatuated with horses. I drew them, dreamt about them, and even pretended at times I *was* one. I had quite an imagination. And today, my father was taking the family to the horse track. All the way there I envisioned what it would be like to see so many majestic creatures all in one place! My heart was racing.

We settled into the bleachers, about half way up, and waited for the races to begin. I was amazed at how crowded it was just to watch horses run. My dad, however, explained that people were there to play a grown-up game called "betting." After hours of watching my dad bet and lose, I lost interest. My sister and I turned our attention to some kids playing below us, who also apparently decided it was enough.

Getting the approval of our parents, we left the adult games behind to pursue our own.

Joining the children on a cement patch, we ran around with delight, until we noticed a chained fence in front of us, separating the bleacher area from the race track. I'm not sure who decided it would be fun to sit on that fence, but before long all the kids were on top like a flock of birds taking a rest. Because I was short, it took me much longer than the others to reach the top. In fact, just as I reached my destination and settled in, the security guards came by and told us we needed to get down. One by one the kids started jumping and running off to congregate in another area. I also wanted to get down quickly and join them, but I hesitated. Climbing that fence was strenuous. Now, sitting so high up, it looked like an enormous feat for me to jump, and because I had a tendency to be a little clumsy, I was scared. Ok, I'll be honest…I am a HUGE klutz. Of course I didn't want the others to know that, and I certainly didn't want to be labeled a baby or a chicken. Even at 8, I had some pride. So I scooted into position and took the leap. As I landed on the pavement, the wind shifted and a gusty breeze blew across me. I was afraid it would throw me off balance, but I landed perfectly on my feet. I was so proud. I had accomplished what the other kids had done with ease—or so I thought.

Suddenly my mother started yelling from the bleachers, as well as other onlookers pointing their fingers at me. It seemed like chaos. Turning around, I realized the sudden breeze I felt was not a wind shift at all. There I stood with my loose fitting shorts ripped all the way to the elastic, exposing my underwear! Apparently, my shorts got hung up on that fence and when I jumped…well, I didn't come out of that situation as unscathed as I originally thought.

At this point, all the kids had turned around to see my shorts flapping in the breeze, like a flag caught high in a gust of wind. Hundreds of people on those bleachers also were observing this spectacle which was more than I could bear. I was extremely embarrassed and for the rest of the afternoon I sat by my mom, a sweater tied across my waist to hide my backside.

Fences—they were never meant to be sat on.

So why in the world are there so many people straddled on them? I'm sure we can all admit at one time or another we too have become fence straddlers. Here are two which I have found to be a common pitfall for many people.

The Fence of Fear

I don't think anyone actually wants to be in a place where they struggle to go forward when God speaks, but often fear will put them in an unsettled place. They know in their heart what to do, but they can't seem to make up their minds to actually do it. How many people do you know who often talk about their dreams for ministry, or life, but never make a move, even when the opportunity presents itself? They are afraid to make a decision and so the answer to them is simple: just don't make one. Fear grips their hearts and entices them to sit upon the fence where action never comes, casually watching the horses go by…never taking a risk, or placing a bet.

Now we have all had our moments when we were indecisive because of fear, but stay upon that fence too long and it will provide a means for you to *live* there as well. I don't know about you, but I find life already passes by too quickly; I don't care to waste any of its precious moments. It would be an awful revelation to look back on life and realize it was full of regrets.

That's why it is important to realize there are seasons when God will literally pour out His favor upon us and push the doors of opportunity wide open. When this occurs, it is usually a short span of time. We have to be able to move without panicking, or at least move in faith DESPITE the anxiety we feel. How many times in the Bible has God said, "Fear not!" as He declares an open door for His people? He wouldn't say not to fear if there wasn't something to be afraid of!

But when God declares, "Fear not!" He is informing you that He will be with you…so move! Now don't misunderstand me. I'm not talking about moving when you don't have any clear direction. I'm talking about not becoming paralyzed when God has made it clear to you in what direction to go!

A good example in the Bible is the story of the Israelites found in *Numbers 13*. God does one miracle after the other for these folks! He takes them out of slavery, leads them through the wilderness, and tells them He is giving them a land full of milk and honey.

There they are at the border when an invisible fence of fear appears. All they have to do is cross over; God was giving them an open door to a beautiful and fertile land. However, instead of concentrating on all that was good, they focused on one thing: GIANTS. Doubts increased and filled their minds and hearts with negativity. Out of their own mouths came derogatory remarks like, "The land is fertile nevertheless…"

That one word, "nevertheless," in the King James Version actually means "in spite of." It's an accusatory remark insinuating that though God promised a fertile land, the odds against them left no hope or possible means of possessing it—despite what the LORD may have said.

Knowing that God is not a man that He should lie, I find this to be a pretty hefty accusation against the LORD! Do you think He doesn't know the obstacles standing in the way? If He has promised something, we can be assured He has a plan on how to make it happen, despite any obstacles we encounter!

In the end, it wasn't the giants that were the problem or their supposed inaccessible cities. The Israelites' demise was because of their FOCUS. The spies tell the people, *"And there we saw the giants, the sons of Anak, which come of the giants: and <u>we were in our own sight as grasshoppers, and so we were in their sight</u>" (Numbers 13:33 KJV)*.

They allowed themselves to be intimidated. This in turn caused their perception of themselves to be quite small in comparison to the giants. In fact, they saw themselves as small as grasshoppers. In turn, the enemy saw the

Israelites exactly how they saw themselves. Had their focus been on God, history would have been written quite differently.

We find in our reading of this story, there were twelve spies that were commanded to go and search out the land. Out of the twelve, only two focused on God. Caleb and Joshua saw the land through the LORD's eyes. God said possess the land and in their estimation nothing else mattered! However, the others saw it through eyes of fear. The sad part is these spies were all leaders.

One would think that by being chosen as a leader of this great nation, it would mean that the leader spent good quality time knowing the LORD. His devotion to God should have caused him to exhale the words of faith to the people. But instead, it was dread and horror which poured out from the hearts of the leaders and they led the majority of the people right into rebellion. The Israelites turned what should have been a night of victory, into a night of crying and bitter grumbling against Moses and the LORD.

Because of this tragic mistake of disobedience, the men who spread the bad report were struck down with a plague before the LORD (*Numbers 14:37*). God also spoke to Moses regarding the rebellious people. He said, "*In this wilderness your bodies will fall—every one of you twenty years old or more who was counted in the census and who has grumbled against me. Not one of you will enter the land I swore with uplifted hand to make your home, except Caleb son of Jephunneh and Joshua son of Nun" (Numbers 14:29-30 NIV).*

After Moses told the people all God had spoken, they arose in the morning saying, *"Now we are ready to go up to the land the Lord promised. Surely we have sinned" (Numbers 14:40 NIV)!* But it was too late! Moses warned them that if they went, they would go alone, because the LORD would not be with them. Sadly, they went anyway. The outcome? They got whooped!

Talk about looking back on life with regrets. They were so close. But they chose to focus in on the problem rather than the solution. Instead of believing God despite what they SAW, they choked! And that is what kept them out. God only allowed the two that believed Him, Caleb and Joshua, and the descendants of that generation, to enter in. Everyone else died in the wilderness, never to experience God's perfect plan for their life *(Numbers 26:65)*.

When God speaks clearly to you, don't allow fear to hinder you from moving. Get your focus on the LORD and trust Him for a victorious end! Don't hesitate to the point that you end up like the Israelites—missing your blessing!

And if you are presently in a place where a decision must be made and God hasn't spoken clearly to you yet, confidently know He is on your side, if you believe and trust in Him! Our Heavenly Father will provide you the open doors and will walk with you every step of the way. He won't leave you clueless! Don't sit on the fence of fear. Quiet your heart and listen; He has the answer.

Here are some incredible guidelines to protect you and help you through the decision making process.

- *"The wise also will hear and increase in learning, and the person of understanding will acquire skill and attain to sound counsel [so that he may be able to steer his course rightly]" (Proverbs 1:5 AMP).*
- *"Lean on, trust in, and be confident in the LORD with all your heart and mind and do not rely on your own insight or understanding" (Proverbs 3:5 AMP).*
- *"Where there is no counsel, purposes are frustrated, but with many counselors they are accomplished" (Proverbs 15:22 AMP).*
- *"Let the peace of Christ be in control of your heart (for you were in fact called as one body to*

this peace), and be thankful" (Colossians 3:15 NET).

During critical moments of decision, if you will take the time to search into God's Word, the Holy Spirit will begin to shed light in areas where it appears a little cloudy. Also, counseling with Godly, faith-filled people regarding major decisions in your life can bring the clarity you need as you wait on the LORD to reveal His plan. I have often looked at situations through a very narrow lens until I have sought advice from others who I respected. They can help you to visualize things differently, making the LORD's plans sometimes easier to see. It also brings a peace and assurance to your heart when you make God the source of your decision.

Sometimes we must take a short period of time to sort out the best answers in our choices, but don't use that as an excuse for procrastination…there is a big difference. It would be tragic indeed to straddle the fence of fear and miss the opportunities life holds for you. Just **SEEK** to follow his guidelines!

The acronym **SEEK**, illustrates a solid pathway for overcoming fear.
1) **S**eek counsel.
2) **E**xercise the truth in God's word.

3) **E**xpect God to guide you as you totally lean on him.
4) **K**eep the Peace of Christ in control of your heart.

Remember: God knows the correct path for your life and He will not fail to show you if you will trust in Him. Don't be a fence straddler, for your next blessing may be right around the corner! Just follow the **S.E.E.K.** pattern and purpose in your heart to run after the promises of God despite the obstacles you may see!

The second principle of fear is quite different from the first fence-straddler, but has the same ability to immobilize faith and thwart your progress in seeking God's favor. The second principle of fear can be learned through that of the gated community.

The Fence of the Gated Community

It is said gated communities are becoming increasingly more popular, and not just for the wealthy. The reason for their increased popularity is "safety." Most gated communities are separated from the outside and require some type of security or key card to gain access. This means less crime and solicitation than normal communities. Those living behind these fences also boast of a cleaner environment and social benefits. As is mentioned in an article from *USA Today* by Haya el Nassar, the common desire among residents is to provide a safe environment for their children and to live among people who share similar values.

God has provided a gated community for believers. However, His community is NOT created to keep undesirables out, but to provide a place for us to obtain encouragement and support from others who share our same values as believers in Christ.

In *Psalm 23*, the LORD is described as a Great Shepherd who leads His sheep to safe pastures. His Word serves as a guideline to keep us guarded within those protective walls made from His grace. But some aren't committed enough to God to be completely sold out, to stay in the protective enclosure He has written, and not reckless enough to be totally in the world. So they sit on that fence in their gated community called a "church."

I have found that these types of half-hearted Christians are restless, and are never quite satisfied or content where they are at in life. There on the fence, they won't come in too deep within the community, so they basically just live on the edge. They come in late to church and slip out early. They are afraid to get too involved or to make any commitments. However, they want to at least live enough within the borders of the church to feel spiritually "safe." Because they never take a risk and jump in, they often find themselves feeling unsettled and disconnected from those they should be a part of.

The struggles they face on a daily basis keeps them isolated. One week they are in the world filling themselves with the sinful desires that lure them away; and the next week they are in the church trying to shake off the darkness, longing for more of God. They don't realize that everyone in the gated community has struggled from time to time, so they keep their struggles hidden rather than seeking the help and support they need. Sitting on the fence in the gated community, they remain isolated by their own lack of involvement, rather than coming in deep to enjoy the benefits of fellowship waiting within. And because temptations keep pulling them away, often condemnation and guilt fill their hearts as well, keeping them up at night. Because of this, fence-straddlers can't truly confess:

"I will both lie down and sleep in peace, for You alone, Lord, make me live in safety" (Psalms 4:8 HCSB).

Living on the fence may give people a sense of safety but it really is a danger and needs to be addressed more often in church.

Rev 3:15-14 (NIV) puts it this way… *"These are the words of the Amen, the faithful and true witness, the ruler of God's creation. I know your deeds, that you are neither cold nor hot. I wish you were either one or the other! So, because you are lukewarm—neither hot nor cold—I am about to spit you out of my mouth.*

God's warnings are not to frighten or condemn us, but to jolt us back into the right position. Sitting on the fence, plain and simple, is nothing more than dangerous living. Whether it's a fence of fear or a fence bordering the gated community, they both accuse God of not being trustworthy in all that He promises His people.

We must not allow our hearts to be filled with fear or half-hearted devotion. Inhale deeply into your spirit, so you can embrace God's grace and promises for your life! And when you do, you will surely exhale the faith to conquer!

Be Encouraged! For God says:

So do not fear, for I am with you; do not be dismayed, for I am your God. I will strengthen you and help you; I will uphold you with my righteous right hand.
(Isaiah 41:10 NIV)

Think About It!

1.   Did you ever straddle a real fence? What was the true reason why it was built?

2.   Have you ever allowed fear to cause you to hesitate on a decision or on moving when God told you to? Did you allow that fear to cause you to miss out on God's blessings, or did you finally get the courage to move?

3.   Is there someone you know who struggles with sin and because of this, refuses to get too close to others in church? How can you help to draw them in?

4.   How can we, as the church, become a "safe" community for others?

Write About It!

Chapter Three

The Groundskeeper

I kill plants. I'm not a purposeful assassin; it just happens. I really do love all the beautiful flowers surrounding my house. The problem is I forget they need attending to. It's not until my flowers droop over with brown shriveled leaves that I realize they haven't had a drink in a while. That's when I try to water them, but I'm never quite sure how much to give. Often, what I intended to be a sprinkle turns into a flood. Sadly, it's obvious by looking at my flower bed, that most plants can't handle this abuse of extreme drought followed by a downpour of rain.

Approximately five years ago, my friend Vicki, showed up at my door with plants galore! She took it upon herself to plant beautiful arrangements for me around my house. I was amazed at how much she liked to get down in the dirt to weed and plant—it just came so natural to her. Now every spring I find a gorgeous array of flowers in my yard. Many times Vicki will stop by to water or weed to keep them alive! And although I don't usually see Vicki when she is working in my yard, I find myself blessing her and praying for her family every time I walk by the wonderful display of colors.

My precious friend blesses me every year with plants, but I still have to learn to maintain what she has given me! I admit that it is quite a challenge for me to keep them alive and Vicki, as well as my family, would probably be the first to tell you I couldn't handle a bigger flower bed. Even now, either my husband or son intervenes at some point so my garden isn't completely desolate! What it comes down to is this: someone has to tend the garden if anything is to survive. Honestly, that someone shouldn't be me!

In *Exodus 23:29-30 (AMP)*, God is getting ready to give the Israelites the land He had promised them. But He warns them beforehand He is not going to drive out the enemy entirely, nor give them the full acreage of land all at one time. There is a good reason for this. God says, *"I will not drive them out from before you in one year, lest the land become desolate (for lack of attention) and the wild beasts multiply against you. Little by little I will drive them out from before you, until you have increased and are numerous enough to take possession of the land."*

God is a strategist! Everything He does is for a purpose and He works on our behalf with great care and intent. The Israelites would not have been able to maintain all of the land God was blessing them with. The Lord made this clear. Therefore, He would allow the Israelites' enemies to remain in certain portions of the land until the Israelites WERE ready. You see, it was critical to the LORD that the Israelites not only receive the land, but *possess* it as well. One of the definitions of possess, according to Merriam-Webster Dictionary, is "to seize and take control of." If they did not literally have control of the entire land, there would be a great danger of it becoming desolate or overrun by dangerous animals due to the lack of attention. God would give them a little at a time so they would have the ability to eventually increase in numbers and expand across the land.

This scripture is a beautiful depiction of what God does for us in every aspect of our lives. He understands there are some things we just can't handle. Whether it is trials or blessings, we need God to intervene and assure us the victory. In this case, the Israelites needed God's involvement in order for the land they were given to **remain** a blessing. You see even blessings can become an unbearable trial if it is too big for us to handle.

This is a good point to remember, because sometimes we complain when the requests we bring to God aren't answered immediately as we would like. It may be praying for an unsaved spouse or a wayward child. It could be our finances or a job that is stressful. Whatever the prayer, seeing glimmers of hope followed by negative outcomes can cause us to become disheartened. If we are honest, we will admit that we just don't want to see little trickles here and there of our prayers being answered; we want a literal downpour…a flood-like victory! This is why the most frustrating times in our lives are often after we have prayed for years and finally see something which looks like a miracle at our door, only to have that situation take a turn for the worse.

It's during those times you might be tempted to say, "Why do I always go one step forward and two steps back in this situation?" You may feel like the enemy is stealing what accomplishments you have gained in the situations you face. I know I have had my share of those kinds of thoughts, but recently the LORD has challenged me in this area.

First of all, if we gain ground in a trial and then suddenly feel the pressure of attacks…why do we assume we have lost ground? When the LORD gave the Israelites the land, He purposely gave them only <u>portions</u> at a time. They needed to possess that portion *first*, and then once that was accomplished, God would give them increase.

Did you ever think that the prayers you prayed, God **was** answering; but only a "little at a time?" Many who pray fervently for healing or restoration, especially in the area of broken relationships; find little glimpses of slight breakthrough followed by great disappointment. I have experienced this even in my own life.

Although we may be quick to blame the devil, this does not necessarily mean he has the upper hand! It is God who is giving you "portions" of breakthrough and asking you to "possess" it before He gives you more. Any pressure or attacks you may feel at the time, is simply a challenge from the enemy. But it is also an opportunity to stand your ground. When God knows you are ready to gain more, He will call you forward and drive the devil back. However, your adversary is hoping to trick you into thinking just the opposite of what is actually happening. He wants you to walk away in defeat, thinking you have lost ground; when in actuality it is just the devil's pressure of resistance as God calls you forward to increase.

I fear many of us have given ground away through a lack of understanding. Rather than moving forward and "possessing" at this critical time when God is pushing the enemy back, we have let it slip away through our attitudes, actions and words. We need instead, to learn how to protect the precious seed of our prayers.

A great example would be found in the life of a farmer. The farmer breaks up the ground in preparation to receive the seed. He plants the seed and then covers it back over with dirt. He then makes sure the plants are watered and cared for. The farmer doesn't go back and dig up the seed after it has been planted to see if it's "working." He has *faith* that what he has sown will produce over time.

When you take your circumstance and plant it into the depths of God's grace through prayer, you should expect results. Every time you speak critically against what you have just prayed, it is as though you are exposing the seed and removing it from the spiritual ground in which you placed it in. It is like inhaling God's precious grace in the secret place of prayer only to exhale destruction…this should not be.

For instance, say there is a mother who has a wild teenager. The mother prays constantly for her child to change. Each night she kneels down at her bed and prays blessings over her child, laying her requests by faith, before the Lord. In those moments it is like a breath of fresh air. She literally breathes in the grace of God; filling her heart with hope. The next morning however, the mother gets up to find her child has the same rebellious and stubborn attitude. Frustrated, the mother begins to wonder if her desperate prayers of the previous night were in vain. Suddenly, she exhales not faith filled words but rather a barrage of destructive ones. She begins to scream at her teen with a loose tongue. "You will never amount to anything!" she says. "I don't know why I even waste my time talking to you." In that moment, it is as though she went back to the seeds she had sown and dug them up.

A farmer would never do such a thing! Sometimes he may find certain seedlings not doing well. When this is the case, he will increase his care for it. He will examine it for insects and disease and will make sure the plant is watered well. A farmer would never just give up or pull it out. Never! Instead, he would do everything he possibly could *first* to assure its survival, hoping eventually it would develop into a healthy plant.

This is the attitude we should have with our prayers and requests made to the LORD. It's also the attitude that should pour forth from our everyday thoughts, actions and words.

"A good man brings good things out of the good stored up in his heart, and an evil man brings evil things

out of the evil stored up in his heart. For the mouth speaks what the heart is full of" (Luke 6:45 NIV).

If we are not careful, we may find ourselves saying, "I'll never get that house; I'll never get out of debt; I probably will never get out of this place; I will never find someone to love." Instead of speaking such things, we need to learn how to draw into our spirit the Grace of God, filling ourselves up to overflowing so we can pour out the faith we need during those trying times. That's maturity. That's what produces results.

James 1:2-8 in the Bible Version, *"The Message,"* says it perfectly:

"²Consider it a sheer gift, friends, when tests and challenges come at you from all sides. ³You know that under pressure, your faith-life is forced into the open and shows its true colors. ⁴So don't try to get out of anything prematurely. Let it do its work so you become mature and well-developed, not deficient in any way.

⁵If you don't know what you're doing, pray to the Father. He loves to help. You'll get his help, and won't be condescended to when you ask for it. ⁶Ask boldly, believingly, without a second thought. People who "worry their prayers" are like wind-whipped waves. ⁷Don't think you're going to get anything from the Master that way, ⁸adrift at sea, keeping all your options open."

Whatever you are praying and believing for—be a Groundskeeper. Protect the seed and trust God for the increase. Remember, every bit of advancement you acquire, the enemy cannot stop unless you let him! It may be a fight…struggles may be hard…but you will increase as the Lord promises. Hold the faith and remember:

> *"…let us not be weary in well doing: for in due season, we shall reap, if we faint not."*
> *(Galatians 6:9 KJV)*

Think About It!

1.	Do you think the Israelites ever got discouraged because they wanted all the land God had for them instead of just portions of it?

2.	Has there ever been a time when you were praying for something that seemed impossible to obtain?

3.	Did you ever get frustrated and speak derogatory over the very thing you were praying to the Lord about?

4.	What is the difference between receiving a blessing and possessing a blessing?

5.	What does inhaling God's grace and exhaling faith mean to you?

Write About It!

46

Chapter Four

Uprooted

The Lord knows how to grab your attention. If you allow Him to, He will use the most unpredictable times and places for one of "life's lessons"—at least that is how He works with me. One day I was not feeling well and so I decided to request a vacation day from work. It wasn't enough to keep me in bed; it was just a queasy stomach. I decided to run a few errands and try to relax as much as possible, in the hopes of feeling better.

There in the car, I was enjoying myself as I sang songs to Jesus and worshipped Him for His amazing grace. It was such a peaceful moment, that although I didn't feel the best, I was glad for the day. But suddenly, peace turned to frustration as a cesspool of thoughts concerning a person who hurt me, came smack in the middle of my worship! It felt like someone had dumped out the trash…right into my mind! I became quite distraught about the whole thing. I had forgiven this person multiple times whenever the thoughts came. I was confident bitter feelings were finally dead and buried. So why were these emotions coming up once again to torment me?

I had been taught that the Bible instructs us to "cast down" bad thoughts which are contrary to the Word of God *(2Cor 10:5)*. Yet even after taking those prescribed steps, here I was finding myself struggling once again. As I sat there in my car, I pondered, "Shouldn't this be a one-time deal?" I mean, if we follow the Biblical guidelines for this, shouldn't it work the ***first*** time?

As far as I was concerned, if I had truly forgiven—which I thought I did—then why did my eyes get squinty and my lips get pursed the moment I thought of this certain person? It just didn't make sense and I wanted an answer. So I began to inquire of the LORD.

"Dear Jesus," I said, as I drove down the street, "Why does this person always come up?" I began to cry out with everything in me, "I don't want this Lord! I really want to be set free! I have given them to you so many times over the years and I truly believe I have released all offenses and wounds. So why does that icky feeling always rise up when this person comes to mind?"

A response came immediately and the words I heard in my Spirit were so simple they became profound.

"Because you can't cast out what needs to be uprooted." He responded.

"Say that again?" I said, wondering if I heard right. His words came again into my spirit "Because you can't cast out what needs to be uprooted!"

As I quieted my heart, the Lord began to unfold the answer to me, opening my eyes wide to forgiveness. It was such a simple truth—I was surprised I hadn't seen it before. But then again, the Holy Spirit is the One who leads and guides us. He always has His perfect timing! As I continued to drive in the car, the LORD poured into me the knowledge needed to finally break free from the bitter root of unforgiveness!

I was taken back in my mind to a time I was teaching my children how to spell. I found a wonderful game that I was able to download on my computer. It was simple, but fun enough for my small children. The game started with a spelling word on the screen. Music would then begin to play as one by one, a word would dance across the page to the center. Once it stopped, the child only had a few seconds to decide what they would do with that word. If it was a word that rhymed with the spelling word (i.e. coat, boat), the child was to drag it over and place it underneath the spelling word. If the word did not rhyme (i.e. coat, cat), the child was to drag it to the garbage can. The kids loved it when they won! For me, it was a great way for my children to learn vocabulary words.

God used that simple game to teach me about casting down and uprooting. He reminded me of a scripture that is usually taught in Sunday school for children to memorize. It is found in *Philippians 4:8 (NIV)*; *"Finally, brothers and sisters, whatever is true, whatever is noble, whatever is right, whatever is pure, whatever is lovely, whatever is admirable--if anything is excellent or praiseworthy--think about such things."*

When meditating on this, it dawned on me that the LORD was revealing an answer to stopping offenses dead in their tracks. When little thoughts dance across our mind, like the child's game I bought for my children, they need to fit the category of His Word! If our thoughts line up with *Philippians 4:8,* we are to deposit them into our hearts. If not, they need to go immediately into the garbage can. Like the child's word game, we only have a few seconds to decide.

If we think too long on thoughts that don't fit, or we deposit them into our heart—casting down no longer works. What a revelation! Just then another scripture came to mind!

[14] *"Pursue peace with everyone, and holiness— without it no one will see the Lord. [15] Make sure that no one falls short of the grace of God and that <u>no root of bitterness</u> springs up, causing trouble and by it, defiling many" (Hebrews 12:14-15 HCSB).*

Wow! The answer was now plain before me! A thought not yet planted can be cast down, but a root needs to be plucked up! All these years I was trying to cast down thoughts that were already seeds of bitterness planted in my heart.

I immediately began to ask the LORD to forgive me and I literally declared out loud that I was pulling out that root of bitterness in Jesus's Name regarding that person! Suddenly my heart was overflowing with forgiveness and I felt light and free! I was able to even pray for that person with genuine joy.

I realized that the LORD had orchestrated this day just for this. But God wasn't done; and what happened next startled me. Just as I felt totally free from this particular person, another person came to my mind! God was letting me know I had more roots to pull.

Over the next hour, I cried and prayed as God brought people to my mind…one by one, I uprooted the bitter roots of unforgiveness and then released them to the Father.

Now any thoughts that are not Godly, I cast down immediately before they reach my heart. I know this isn't always easy…our flesh wants to chew on things awhile. But I have learned when I don't heed this principle, I better be ready to have a fight; as bitter roots of the heart, much like dandelions, aren't always easily pulled!

Hosea 4:6 states, God's people are destroyed for a "*lack of knowledge.*" That is why it is important for me to get the word out—to let people know that we can save ourselves years of unforgiveness, offenses and bitter roots. These things are what poison our heart and mind, making us miserable and many times ill.

So next time a bad thought comes your way…play the casting down game and send it to the garbage can for a win!

Think About It!

1. Have you ever genuinely forgiven someone only to find negative thoughts popping up once again in your mind?

2. When bad thoughts about someone come, do you immediately cast them down, or have you found yourself replaying hurtful memories again and again?

3. Have you ever become sick to your stomach from confrontations that caused offenses? Did you seek to resolve the ill will that came between you and others, or did you just try to forget it?

4. What is the most important difference between "casting down" imaginations and thoughts contrary to the Word and "uprooting them?"

Write About It!

Chapter Five

Voices from the Graveyard

Looming in the darkness they call. At times their voices are weak and distant, while other times close and forceful. These are the shadows of your past, beckoning you back to a place long ago.

The Word of God clearly states when you come to accept the LORD, the slate is wiped clean. *"For if a man belongs to Christ, he is a new person. The old life is gone. New life has begun" (2Cor 5:17 NLV).*

When I look back on my life—between the old Lisa and the new, the differences are so vast it seems like I'm looking at two totally different people...and I am. The lifestyle I lead is nothing like my life before Christ and that is the way it is for most of us who have decided to follow Him.

But there are times when the haunting voices of sin try to entice us back to a sinister world of destruction:

- Idle men, who once were on fire for God, suddenly hear the voices of temptation luring them back to pornography. Though they are Christians, seeking to honor God, they sit by their computers, isolated and alone. Suddenly an unexpected picture pops up on the screen...then the voices come. Speaking to their fleshly desires, they know the sensual world of their past is only one click away. Their hand is upon the mouse, their finger in place—"just click it!" the voice says.

- Then there is the girl who loves Jesus, yet still struggles with insecurities. She longs for a man to hold her, to show her she matters, even if it means once again giving herself away. She remembers the lies, the false promises these men told her, but they call to an empty part within her soul, broken and in need of love.

- People who find their Christianity becoming boring and stale, suddenly hear the memories of laughter; friends gathered at a party they had attended years ago. Their mind recalls those times as exuberant and fun, unlike the drab life they now lead. They pick up the phone to dial an old friend from the past and think,

"What will it hurt to just go out ONE time?"

Though these samples may seem drastic, the scenarios happen every day. Some of you may find yourself stronger than that…you would never go back to the old life you say. But what about the sins of the present? You promised you wouldn't get angry anymore, gossip any more, overeat anymore, pop the top to a beer can or light a cigarette…the list goes on. Yet the struggles are still there urging you to come back to the habits you thought you crucified.

1Corinthians 10:15 (HCSB) states, *"No temptation has overtaken you except what is common to humanity. God is faithful, and He will not allow you to be tempted beyond what you are able, but with the temptation He will also provide a way of escape so that you are able to bear it."*

According to the scriptures the steps should be as simple as this: (1) temptation comes, (2) God shows you how to get out of the situation, and (3) you take the escape route, beating the enticement and securing a great victory! Sounds easy, right? Not quite.

Allurement of sin is many times unpredictable. It can happen in good times or bad. And though no one likes to admit it, we are all vulnerable to being drawn in. The Bible states no temptation has overtaken you that is not uncommon to man. Per Merriam-Webster Dictionary, the definition of overtaken means "to catch up and pass while traveling in the same direction, or something that comes suddenly or un-expectantly." In other words, temptation can slowly chip away at your defenses until it draws you into its clutches; or it can present itself as a sudden urge. Either way it seems to be a lot easier beating sin in the textbook than in actual practice; all because of one thing: our fleshly cravings.

Though each one of us has our individual weakness, let's be honest—you know your trigger point! And when that trigger goes off, the intense battle begins. A battle that rages like a tidal wave within your mind!

The Word says God will provide a way of escape so we can beat the temptation without succumbing to it; so why do we still find ourselves falling prey? The answer is easier than what you would believe. It's because we give ourselves time to THINK about the sin rather than heading for the nearest exit! Allowing your mind to engage with the voices and thoughts of sin, even for a moment, will drag you over the boundary where you won't want an out...at least not until sin has been satisfied and remorse sets in.

I found a beautiful story of God's resurrection power and a secret, I believe, to fighting sin. It is found in *John 11:44*. Jesus's friend, Lazarus, died. When Jesus arrived, he had already been buried in the tomb for 4 days and the stench of decay had set in. But Jesus miraculously calls Lazarus back from the dead. The scripture states, *"And Lazarus came—bound up in the grave cloth, his face muffled in a head swath. Jesus told them, "Unwrap him and let him go" (John 11:44 TLB)!*

What is interesting to me in this story is found in the end; when Jesus tells the friends and family gathered by the tombstone, "Unwrap him and let him go!"

You see, Jesus displayed His glorious resurrection power when he called Lazarus out of the tomb; but Lazarus was still wrapped up like a mummy! It took people around him to take off those grave cloths. Having others remove what bound Lazarus, did not diminish Jesus's miraculous feat of raising him up from the dead. Yet it does reveal that even after such a supernatural work, there still is some work left to be done.

When we come to know Jesus, we are raised out of the grave of sin and death. God then resuscitates us with His Spirit, giving us new life in Him. According to *2Corinthians 5:17*, our old life is gone. However, as we move into this new life Christ has given us, we soon realize we too, like Lazarus, still have some grave clothes on. Removing these death rags becomes vital to our wellbeing; for even the stench of sin clinging to us can tempt us back into the graveyard.

Which brings us to an important point. Sometimes, in order to remove everything still binding us, we must be willing to allow others to help. This is done by permitting Christian friends to teach us how to live, to pray with us for strength when we are weak, and even to hold us accountable when we need it.

My son-in-law, Caleb is a very special man. He has an incredible loyalty and love for his friends. Anyone who knows him will tell you they are blessed to have him in their lives.

At least Glenn would tell you it is so. He was someone who hung out quite often with Caleb and his friends. Glenn was a new Christian, but he had a great zeal for the LORD.

Soon he began to get involved with Caleb and the others in a Christian rap ministry, reaching out to the community. Their work was going strong and God was using them mightily. They kept each other accountable and gathered together often for prayer and Bible studies. Things were going well, until one dark day, when Glenn found himself back in the grips of his old life.

One Saturday morning my daughter woke up and told Caleb she felt like she was grieving, as though someone was going to die. They both thought it was very strange, but they brushed it off and got ready for the day.

Within 30 minutes, Glenn's wife, Maria called. She was worried. There was money missing from the house and Glenn never came home last night. She said she felt a strange foreboding of death.

That was enough of a confirmation for them all. There was an urgency to find Glenn and find him quick! But where would they look? Milwaukee is a huge city and they had no idea where to start.

After praying, they literally jumped in the car and desperately drove not knowing where to go. Caleb randomly turned down one street and then another, when Maria saw a man staggering down the road. She rolled down the window, not knowing who he was and yelled, "Hey, where's Mo?"

Caleb thought, "Who is Mo?" but then realized it was Glenn's old street name.

"He's in there." the ragged man said pointing to the house in front of them.

Could this really be happening? Glenn could have been anywhere in the city making the odds of finding him impossible. Yet God led Caleb and Maria's actions in such a way that they ended up right in front of the drug house where Glenn was!

My daughter stayed in the car while Maria and Caleb went in and she immediately called my husband and me for prayer. I have to admit, we were afraid when we found out what was going on. My husband knew the Milwaukee streets well, and no one just walks into a drug house! The events playing out this night were just insane…or purely miraculous.

As soon as they walked in, a man started to yell at them, but Maria threatened to call the cops. Now Caleb and Maria both were street wise; they knew threatening to call the police in a drug house was probably the number one most dangerous thing to say! But Maria, having prayed most of the night for Glenn, was operating under the unction of the Holy Spirit. There was power and authority in her voice, which caused the man to panic.

"Come right in!" he said.

They found Glenn in a small room towards the back of the house. He was a mess. He was so drugged up that his eyes were actually rolling back. He was extremely high, but was still able to recognize Caleb. He was quite embarrassed to realize his Christian brother was there to see him doing drugs again. Caleb and Maria lifted Glenn up and made their way towards the door.

Things got intense. The man that first met them when they walked in, began cussing and calling Maria bad names, telling Glenn he didn't have to listen to a woman. It was as though he was the devil himself as he began to appeal to Glenn's pride, beckoning him back.

In that moment, Glenn came to his senses. Hearing the violent words spewing from the man's mouth, Glenn turned around and spoke as though God was speaking through him.

The man threw up his hands in defeat and backed away.

Caleb and Maria placed Glenn into the back seat of his car and Caleb got into the driver's seat. He instructed Maria to go home with my daughter while he stayed with Glenn.

As Caleb drove, Glenn, being a large man, reached around the entire front seat and began hugging Caleb. Weeping bitterly, he kept saying he couldn't believe how much Caleb cared…that he would actually take the time to search for him.

It was a dangerous act of love!

Once they were far enough away, Caleb picked up some Gatorade to rehydrate his friend and then parked the car so they could talk. They sat there for a long time as Caleb lovingly spoke to Glenn about the importance of changing.

That night, Caleb literally removed the grave clothes of sin off of his friend and walked him out of the graveyard of drugs. Glenn truly saw the redemption story of Jesus played out before his eyes.

Because of this one night of relentless love, Glenn never returned to that graveyard. He is on fire for Jesus today and is more passionate than he ever was before. He now spends his time reaching out to those on the streets, who struggle like he once did.

We have been resurrected by the sacrifice of Christ's blood. We are the redeemed ones, those filled with His Power and Grace. We don't have to listen to the voices creeping in the shadows calling us back! We have an immediate escape route provided by our loving Father. He gives us whatever is necessary to ensure our victory; including friends willing to help remove the dead things of our past. The LORD promises, in *Revelation 12:11,* we will overcome by the blood of the Lamb and by the word of OUR testimony!

Let us rejoice, for we have an amazing Heavenly Father, and a loving family found in the Body of Christ. Let us help one another to remove the grave clothes of our past and run the race with excellence!

Pray with me:

Lord, help us to be the light, dispelling the darkness which beckons others to their old life of sin. Let us seek to remove the grave cloths remaining and show Your love by our relentless efforts. Let us be the tool You use to rescue those finding themselves in the graveyard once again. Amen.

Think About It!

1. The devil knows you better than you think. He knows exactly what scenarios to place in your path that will trigger temptation. Thinking about the sins you are prone to struggle with, what are some things that set you off?

2. Have you ever noticed a time in your life where a blessing, because it was not handled correctly, turned into a temptation or curse?

3. Think of the last time you were tempted. What was the way of escape that God provided? Did you take it, or give in to your flesh? How did you feel after the fact?

4. Some of God's greatest blessings are Godly friendships. He uses those relationships to encourage and comfort us, and sometimes to help keep us in line. Was there ever a time where a Godly friend had to confront you about your sin? How did you receive this correction?

Write About It!

Chapter Six

Dr. G

Dr. John A. Goeckermann was listed among the top ten in the nation for Oral & Maxillofacial Surgery. It wasn't hard to understand why. He was not only intelligent surgically, but had business savvy as well. He was an incredible man that was liked by everyone; and I had the great privilege of being his office manager for over 11 years.

Our families came to know each other on a personal basis as well. My two girls worked for him for several years and his boys would come over during summer vacation to help. We had a blast during those times. The office was always filled with laughter.

Dr. G, as we called him, lived life to the fullest. I never saw such energy in one person. Every weekday he was in the gym by 5 a.m. and would come barreling into the office at the last minute, right before his first patient. During lunch and after work there was usually more running around, whether it was activities with the family or meetings with the doctors. He never seemed to stop.

Dr. G had purchased land and had a new building made to his specifics. I loved the new place and was able to have an office in the front near the hub of activity. His office was built way in the back where he could concentrate on his chart notes. His dream was to eventually have his oldest son, who was in school for Oral Surgery, join him as a partner.

One day, however, Dr. G came in a little worn out. He said he had pulled a muscle in the gym several weeks ago and had been taking medication for the pain. He suffered a few weeks more and then decided he needed to get it checked out. That was the first time I really ever saw him feeling ill, other than maybe a slight cold from time to time.

I will never forget that dark day when he called all of us to the reception area for a staff meeting. He looked quite solemn and dread filled my heart…something was wrong. He started his conversation the way he often did—telling us how much he loved us and appreciated our commitment and hard work. But his next words out of his mouth felt like someone had slammed me in the gut and I couldn't breathe. Dr. G had cancer.

He tried to assure us he would do everything he could to fight this disease, and he asked us not to leave him. He promised to do whatever he could to help us so no matter the outcome, we weren't left in the end without jobs. That was just like Dr. G, always thinking about those around him. We all agreed without hesitation to stay and we promised to stand by him—for better or worse.

As the months dragged on, I saw Dr. G getting thinner and becoming very pale. One of the hardest trials in life is to see someone you care about slowly dying before your eyes. I was concerned for my friend's life, but even more for his salvation. He was a good man and a religious man…but did he know the LORD in a personal way? That was a question that constantly gnawed at my soul.

I prayed for him fervently every day and for his wife Carol, as well as the children. On days when Dr. G was weak, he would go into the last surgical room near his office and lay down. He never used that room anyway, so it was the perfect place to rest in between seeing his patients. He wasn't giving up and I appreciated that about him. He was a fighter. But he never wanted people to see his struggle. He would rise up from the chair and go into the surgical room where the patient was. Grinning from ear to ear, he would make his usual, corny jokes and assure them that he would take care of whatever oral issue they were having. Many never knew there was something wrong. Some days, I would walk into his office when he wasn't expecting it and I would see him cringing in pain. Of course, as soon as he saw me he would smile trying to hide it. I would gently put my hand on his and say, "Are you o.k.?" In which he always replied, "Of course. I'm fine!" I knew better.

On Tuesdays, Dr. G was always at the hospital performing surgeries. That is when I took advantage of praying in the room where he would lay down. I would put soft Christian music on, hoping the LORD's healing and peace would rest in the room. I could feel a tangible presence of God there, which made me confident…Dr. G would be healed!

That day came when it appeared that our prayers were answered! Dr. G came popping into my office with a big smile on his face and sat on the credenza near my desk. "Guess what?" he asked with a huge smile. With great delight he shared how his doctor said his last blood count numbers were so good, if he didn't personally know the situation, he would never even think he had cancer. He then pumped his arm into his side saying, "Yes!"

I saw several months go by where Dr. G had his energy back and I was rejoicing for the miracle of his healing. God was actually doing this! He was definitely our Healer and our Savior. But then our worst nightmare came—Dr. G got sick. It was cold season and he ended up with a virus which suddenly turned his condition for the worse. Days later he came back into my office and sat upon that same credenza he had so many months ago. But this time it was without his precious smile. "Promise me, Lisa." he said seriously. "Anything." I replied. With saddened eyes he spoke, "Take care of Carol. Help her with the business and make sure she is ok." I wanted to scream, "No! You will get well." But I knew this was too important for him. "Absolutely." I replied, "I promise."

The last time I sat in his office, his wife Carol was there. He was exhausted and full of sorrow as he shared the dreaded news that the cancer had spread throughout his body and had metastasized to his liver. I was numb. This just couldn't be happening.

He slowly rose from his desk to go see his next patient and grabbed my hand. "Just pray that I would have courage Lisa…just pray for courage."

Soon after he was bedridden, and although no one was allowed to visit at that time,

Carol welcomed Carlos and me over to the house. I was grateful, but anxious as we drove there, wondering what we would say. I was in constant prayer, asking the LORD that if He was going to take Dr. G, He would at least show us that he was ready.

I had noticed the last several months that there was a change in his countenance…a peace he didn't have previously. I remember him telling me that his priest had given him a book on peace that was very helpful to him. I had hoped it brought him closer to the LORD at this moment when he needed Him most. I would soon find out.

I didn't know what to expect, but I was secretly struggling for some time with the whole situation. I was angry, and I found myself crying out to God with subtle accusations, though I didn't want to admit it.

"God, you are supposed to be faithful." I would say. Suppose to be—"Why aren't you?" is what my heart was really saying. I just didn't understand. I felt His presence in that surgical room where I prayed. I saw Dr. G get better. Why then was this happening? Why?

When Carlos and I walked into his home and into his bedroom, there was Dr. G sitting in bed. He had a big smile on his face and began to love on us with his words. "Thanks for coming…I love you guys so much…thanks for being such a wonderful family and friends and allowing me to be a part of your lives!" We wanted to minister to him, but he was ministering to us and saying his goodbyes.

It was strangely wonderful. God's presence was so strong there. Our intentions when coming was to ask Dr. G if he was ready to meet His Savior, but in that moment we didn't have to. It was obvious. God was not only there in a tangible way, but you could see Jesus in his eyes.

The next time we came to visit it was on a Wednesday and he had already slipped into a coma. Carol and I talked awhile and we prayed for him, but I wondered—what do you say in a time like this? What words could possibly help? There were none that I could think of. So I just did what I knew to do, which was to be there for her. I felt her appreciation, and although I wished I could have said or done more, being there was enough.

Saturday morning, I rose up from bed and was going to the bathroom to get ready for the day when an old hymn burst from my mouth, "Great is thy faithfulness! Great is thy faithfulness! Morning upon morning new mercies I see…"

I stopped and took a deep breath. "Lord!" I said, "You took Dr. G home didn't you? He made it, didn't he?"

His reply came to my heart and I could visualize God pointing His finger at me with great passion and gentle admonishment, "You see Lisa—I AM FAITHFUL!"

"Yes you are LORD!" I cried, "Yes you are."

I was ashamed that I mistrusted God so. I felt bad that He had to defend himself to me. Someone who proclaimed His goodness; who felt His love. But it was a lesson I had to learn. I had seen so many people over my lifetime battle with cancer and other life-threatening diseases. Some were healed; others were not. I had come to an understanding that God's love is greater than ours. He has our best interest even in the darkness. It was clear to me now having experienced this journey, that God loves His people more than we ever could. I thought healing Dr. G was God's way of being faithful; the only true way of showing His love.

The truth is, God's love transcends far beyond this world. To heal Dr. G would have been a small thing indeed, compared to His plan for him. To have God transform his life, walk with him through the trials, and then receive him into the wonderful joys of His Glorious

Kingdom is a far greater love…a love He provided for us all on the cross.

I think of those days sometimes and tears come to my eyes. I miss him, but the sting is gone. For I know that Dr. G lives eternally with our Lord and one day, we will meet again.

"Let not your heart be troubled: ye believe in God, believe also in me. ² In my Father's house are many mansions: if it were not so, I would have told you. I go to prepare a place for you. ³ And if I go and prepare a place for you, I will come again, and receive you unto myself; that where I am, there ye may be also."

John 14:1-3 (KJV)

Think About It!

1.   Was there ever a time in your life when things were really going well and then suddenly you received bad news?

2.   Some things in life can change everything. In your circumstance, how did you maintain some normalcy?

3.   Were you able to see small miracles and blessings in the midst of your trial?

4.   Did you ever have the intent to go and minister to someone, but when you got there you realized the LORD had already gone before you?

5.   Have you ever been disappointed or angry with God because things didn't turn out as you thought they would?

6.   After your fiery trial, did you find your faith lessened or increased? How about your trust in God?

Write About It!

Chapter Seven

What's Bugging You?

It was a perfect day to be inspired. At least I thought so. Juggling my laptop, water bottle and phone in my hands, I headed out to my backyard to write another chapter of my book, fully expecting to inhale the wonderful insights God would give me.

I chose the perfect spot to sit, right in the middle of my yard only a few feet from a shaded apple tree. The outdoors always seemed to motivate me and today the weather was absolutely perfect. I was positive there would be no writer's block for me.

However, within minutes a creepy, black spider jumped on my shoulder! Now little fanged creatures may be no big deal to some, but spiders are right up there on my danger list with snakes and scorpions! I immediately jumped up, almost dropping my laptop, and slapped that thing so hard I think I may have knocked it clear into the neighbor's yard!

My heart was beating so fast that it took me a few minutes to calm myself down. Once I did, I took a deep breath and began to write again, reminding myself that I liked the outdoors. After some time, I hit that wonderful writer's groove when I was attacked again—this time by a swarm of gnats! Those pesky insects seemed to have come out of nowhere. I waved my hands frantically around my head and determined I WOULD NOT be bullied!

I chuckled a little at the nonsense I was experiencing and so decided to call my son who often took care of the yard. I teasingly informed him of the bugs which were "bugging me" and suggested he spray something strong to kill them. After all, I was hoping my yard would be a sanctuary of tranquility—the perfect writer's paradise! My son laughed and said he would see what he could do.

I continued to converse with him when I suddenly saw a great big bumble bee come out of our cluster of trees bordering our yard. Wouldn't you know, I was directly in its flight path, and it had no intentions on changing its course. I started to scream at the top of my lungs as I tried batting it away. I could hear my son losing it on the other side of the phone.

"This isn't funny!" I shouted. But his uncontrollable laughter caused me to giggle. I stood in my yard frozen with unbelief, when I glanced up to see a silk worm that literally looked like it was suspended in the air, just in front of my face.

"It's literally hanging right in front of me!" I told my son. "It's doing what?" he questioned.

"I'm telling the truth!" I said, thinking he didn't believe me. "It's flying just a few feet away from me!"

Seriously? This was ridiculous! What are the odds in one half acre of land for all the bugs to congregate directly where I'm sitting? They have an entire yard to play in, not to mention a huge park behind our house—so why in the world are they bugging me?

I rose up the white flag of defeat, packed up my belongings and went into the house to write. Unfortunately, every bit of creativity I had, flew away when the bugs came.

So what's bugging you? In *Song of Solomon 2:15 (HCSB)* it states, *"Catch the foxes for us-- the little foxes that ruin the vineyards—for our vineyards are in bloom."*

The idea here is little, seemingly insignificant things can cause problems; ones which interfere with the good things in life. For me it was literal bugs. But many times in our lives, it's the everyday annoyances tripping us up.

I have often found myself getting disturbed over unexpected things which weren't in my plans. Have a morning starting off with a few mishaps and it can change your attitude for the entire day. Have you ever had a scenario like this: you misplace your keys and are running late for work? You find them barely in time and run out of the house without eating. No problem you think, I will just go through the drive-thru somewhere. You pick up a sandwich and coffee but accidentally spill it all over yourself, as well as the car's upholstery. If that isn't bad enough; someone cuts you off on the highway causing you to almost get into an accident. By the time you get to work, you are totally frazzled and full of grumbling remarks…and the day hasn't even started yet!   The truth is if we concentrate on all that is wrong, we will miss out on all that is right. The Bible describes a story of a woman who was allowing small things to bug her, and because of it she had shut herself off from the amazing things happening right in her home. It is found in *Luke 10:38-42*.

Martha often invited Jesus into her humble abode when he was traveling by. Of course, He always had His disciples with Him, which meant there would be more food to prepare. Martha was like a busy beaver in the kitchen, working hard to be a good hostess, when she notices her sister Mary is just sitting at Jesus's feet. I can imagine Martha getting increasingly upset as she is scurrying around by herself, and finally reaches her boiling point. Thinking she is in the right, she asks Jesus to make her sister help. As far as Martha was concerned, Jesus would certainly agree with her. After all, she was serving others; a lesson He often taught.

But Jesus surprisingly does not take her side in this matter and says, *"Martha, Martha! You worry and fuss about a lot of things. There's only one thing you need [worth worrying about]. Mary has made the right choice, and that one thing will not be taken away from her" (Luke 10:41-42 GW).*

Now I know many women wouldn't admit it, but if they were hosting a party like Martha and weren't getting any help, I can guarantee there would be some ladies who would be pretty bugged about it. After all, Jesus is the main guest and good impressions have to be made.

In defense of Martha, I believe she had a true servant's heart and her preparations were an act of love towards the LORD. The problem was Martha allowed her annoyances to take away from the reason why she was serving in the first place: love. It also took her focus off the most important thing going on in the room; the opportunity to hear deep revelations being taught by Jesus. The Lord lovingly confronts her by saying, "Martha, Martha You worry and fuss about a lot of things…"

Repeating her name twice was an endearing way for Jesus to say He was genuinely concerned for her. It was not a rebuke, but a gentle admonishment to focus on what mattered. He didn't tell her being hospitable was wrong; however, it was clear her attitude was. Martha was grumbling about temporal things as though she was being short changed…getting stuck with work while everyone else enjoyed the fellowship. Yes, food had to be served; but it surely didn't take precedence over the other events of the day. She could have put the plate down, tucked the towel away and sat a moment. Martha had a choice…to choose where she would put her attention. Jesus had life-changing lessons to teach and like Mary, she could have taken the opportunity to drink it in. In the end, all that fussing caused her to miss out on deep truths which the LORD wanted to pour into her. Jesus said there was one thing that was needful and Mary found it: it was gleaning from the presence of God when the opportunity presented itself.

How many opportunities of seeing God's glory have been overlooked by the distractions of the day? I wonder what blessings we are missing simply because we get exasperated by things not going the way we think they should. So next time you find yourself in the midst of annoyances—stop and look around. In that moment, remember you have a choice. You can fuss about all the things bugging you; or you can choose to open your eyes wide to the extraordinary truths and blessings that God is gifting to you.

> *"Do not be anxious about anything. Instead, in every situation, through prayer and petition with thanksgiving, tell your requests to God."*
> *(Philippians 4:6 NET)*

Think About It!

1.   Do you remember a day that seemed to be filled with annoyances?

2.   Did these annoyances change your emotions negatively, or were you able to overcome?

3.   Was there ever a time when you were so zoned into all the little things bugging you, that you actually missed out on something special?

4.   What do you do to help yourself when things are not turning out the way you planned? Are there any scriptures that have strengthened you during those times?

Write About It!

Chapter Eight

The Holding Tank

Sometimes we just need a different perspective; but it's not always easy to get. Especially, when you feel like a fish swimming in a fish bowl.

Have you ever thought about it? I mean life as a fish? There they are swimming in this small container day in and day out. They move right up to the glass, searching for a way out; hoping they will one day go farther—deeper than ever before. But the fish soon realizes after swimming from one side to the other, they are stuck.

I have seen a few fish try to escape their holding tank. Jumping out of the bowl, they found themselves flapping their fins against the table, frantic for the water they needed to survive. It was a bad idea—but I can relate.

Working in a very difficult atmosphere, I have tried to escape to better surroundings only to find myself feeling like that fish out of water: spiritually dry, gasping for more of God, and quite disappointed. But ultimately I did learn valuable lessons from it all. One being that no matter what, God is always in control and always has the last say!

My lessons started one day when I decided I had enough. I knew the LORD placed me where I was at, but in my estimation my "spiritual" job of witnessing to those around me was over. They heard the Gospel for over six years. Some accepted it; most rejected it. So as far as I was concerned, it was time to pack up and be on my way.

I sent my resume to a well-known insurance company and put my friend from church down as a reference. She said this company actually welcomed employee acquaintances and would often put those resumes on top. Sure enough, I was soon called to take two tests that would determine if I would get an interview.

My friend warned me ahead of time that one of the examinations was extremely difficult; people rarely passed it. In fact, she had recommended a handful of friends over the years, but all of them failed. I still believed this was my opportunity from the LORD; so she wished me good luck, and told me she would be praying.

I received my notice for the exam date and scheduled a couple of hours off of work.

With my "professional" clothes in a bag, I couldn't wait to punch out. This would be the day of my deliverance!

When I got downtown to the building, I was instructed to park in their *free* parking lot. However, it was completely full. After driving around for several minutes, I conceded to the fact I would have to go elsewhere and pay. Being down to my last couple of dollars, I was upset about it; but then decided I would make the best of the situation. After all, $10 was a small price to pay for my freedom!

The long and short of the story is this: I passed the incredibly difficult test and failed the easy one. Tell me, how is it possible to flunk a test with multiple choice questions, asking you to choose between answers like this:

"Hi, my name is Lisa Rodriguez. How may I help you?" or "Hello, I am Miss Lisa. How can I be of assistance?"

Yet a test full of mathematical equations and definition of words not commonly used, I pass with flying colors! As the Human Resource Manager told me of my failure, tears filled my eyes. I thanked him for his time and slowly walked back to the car. I was numb…it wasn't supposed to end this way!

My heart was heavy as I drove into my driveway and I made a mad dash to my prayer room to have it out with God.

"Why did you allow me to waste my time?" I complained, "You knew I wasn't going to succeed!"

The LORD remained silent, so I went on. "You know I hate my job," I grumbled, "So why? And what was that all about with the parking lot?" I cried out with anger, "You knew I was down to my last dollars…you could have at least provided the FREE parking space so I wasn't wasting my money!"

On and on I went until at last I took a breath; and then the LORD spoke, "Oh, I see." He said calmly, "So…that was your dream?"

"What?" I exclaimed, "No—I mean—what?—of course it wasn't my dream! NO!"

And then I got it. "LORD! Your right…IT'S NOT MY DREAM!" It hit me. What in the world was I complaining about?

I took fifteen minutes to have a hissy fit and yet God turned my perspective around with one simple question. A question packed with truth! What an astonishing God we serve—and merciful! He didn't rebuke me; He just softly corrected me. What love…what grace! I understood now and believed wholeheartedly God in His mercy blocked me from getting this job. Once again He was being a loving Father who had my best interest at hand.

I took the next hour just praising Him and thanking Him for His wisdom. It was clear I was using this opportunity as a means of escape, to get out of a place I didn't like. But God had bigger plans for me and they didn't include this company.

I'm sure I am not the only one who has felt like a fish stuck in a bowl and has attempted to escape. According to a Gallup Poll taken in 2013, over 70% of people in the world hate their jobs! Seeing many of us spend almost our entire waking time each day at those jobs, it is a sad percentage indeed.

But let me encourage you a moment. Being stuck in a holding tank doesn't mean there isn't more out there for us. We just have to realize it is a temporary place where God prepares and refines us. Now I know when we have our noses up against the tank's glass wall, we get frustrated swimming in the shallowness of the everyday humdrum of our lives. Destiny within us tells us that we were created for more! But don't despair! When we look at the Bible stories, we see multiple people who were in holding tanks for a time, and came out to do powerful things for our God!

I think of Moses whose holding tank was the backside of the desert. It must have been frustrating for him to experience the palace all those years only to find himself in some forgotten wilderness tending sheep. Then there was David, who was anointed by God, yet found himself still stuck in his old job in his father's field. Even years later when it seemed like his destiny was about to be fulfilled, he found himself trapped in the darkness of hidden caves running from a King who held his position—a position God told David was his!

Let's not forget about the women of the Bible too. Ruth was stuck in a strange land gleaning fields as a widow, seemingly poor and desolate. Esther, who desperately needed to seek God for deliverance of her people, found herself in the holding tank of her own chambers, agonizing with a decision which could cost Esther her life.

During those desperate times of confinement, like a fish in a small bowl—these great men and women of God probably wanted the LORD to take His fishing net and scoop them up to a new destination, one that was full of excitement and deliverance. Well, I have some encouraging news! In His timing, He did!

Moses went from the wilderness back to the palace, but this time with the Power and

Authority of God Himself! David went on to be King of Israel and had the favor and blessings of the LORD during his reign. Ruth went from the fields as a widow, to the house of Boaz, becoming his wife and gaining the respect and prosperity she had lost. Esther left her holding chambers and stood before the King. Risking her life, she not only found favor with him, but became an incredible deliverer of her nation!

These are only a few of the mighty people spoken of in the Bible, who went out of a holding tank to fulfill the extraordinary plans of God for their lives. So next time you find yourself feeling like a fish in a fish bowl, remember the holding tank is just one step closer to your destiny. *It is where separation for preparation begins!* Then once your training is over, the LORD will call you out, and lead you into the supernatural workings of His Spirit, providing you with success!

When that happens, everything you went through will make sense, and you will get a whole new perspective on what your holding tank was really for. Even though it was a place that kept you tightly contained, it was a blessing! It was a place where you were taught deep things of God, a place where you were stripped of self so you could one day jump from what seemed like a little fish bowl, to a whole pool of possibilities.

Think About It!

1. Was there ever a time when you prayed so hard for something to happen, and felt sure God was going to answer your prayers?

2. While praying for that situation, did it ever seem circumstances became increasingly worse? Did you feel as though God had turned His back on it or had forgotten you?

3. When and if that situation had finally come to an end, did you find God was indeed faithful, even if circumstances weren't what you had expected or planned?

4. Have you ever gone through something that although disappointing, caused you to understand God's grace in a greater way?

Write About It!

Chapter Nine

When God Speaks

What in the world was going on? Only minutes before, the hallway was crowded with hundreds of students scurrying to their next class. Now I suddenly found myself standing in the middle of an empty corridor...all alone.

I knew there was an exam next hour, but I had no clue what it was for! I opened the folder that was in my hands and shuffled through the papers. I was hoping I would get lucky and find notes hinting to what I should have studied. My heart pounded as I realized I only had a few minutes before the bell would ring.

Out of my peripheral vision I could see a teacher approaching me, however, I was just too full of anxiety to care. He came and stood silently at my side as I continued to flip through the papers. I never raised my head to look at him, but I could see the lower half of his long white robe.

"You better hurry," he said breaking the silence, "You have a test next hour!"

"I know!" I said panicking.

Again he spoke, but with a stern urgency in his voice, "You better hurry...the bell is about to ring."

I was startled as I opened my eyes and realized I had been dreaming about school. I found it quite strange seeing I graduated years ago. In fact, I had been married several years now and was raising a toddler and newborn.

I dressed quickly and ran into the kitchen to speak to my husband. "Carlos," I said," I had a dream I was back in school!"

"Oh...really?" He chuckled, thinking it was going to be a funny story.

"No, Carlos… not the typical crazy dream." I said earnestly. "It was a warning from God and surprisingly, I know what it meant!"

Most dreams like this I would just brush off as a nightmare from my teen days. I never liked school to begin with, so it wasn't uncommon back then to dream about silly things. You know…dreams about not being able to find your classroom or forgetting the combination to your locker. But this was different. This dream was embedded deep within my spirit and I couldn't shake it off. Every detail was so vivid…for a moment, I thought it really happened.

I was absolutely convinced the teacher was our sweet Jesus, warning me of a test coming our way. In the dream, there was an urgency in His voice and a panic in mine. It was clear to me the test was "next hour;" which I took as meaning right around the corner. The most important emotion attached to this dream revealed I was not prepared for it!

I didn't quite understand the magnitude of this situation. I had only been a Christian for a few years, and never experienced something like this before. All I knew is that I was suddenly being compelled by a dream; a dream I knew was from God. I was filled with a great determination and urgency in my heart, calling me to action. I immediately went into a time of fasting and prayer and increased my Bible reading.

Over the next few days, I noticed a peace coming upon me. I felt renewed as though I had inhaled deeply, filling my lungs with a cool summer breeze. I was more awake and alive—full of energy. I also gained a strong confidence and trust in the LORD: an increase of faith.

Then several weeks later, the test I was warned about came. My little daughter, Cecilia, being only two years old at the time, had her bedroom directly adjacent to ours. As a new mom, it made me feel more at ease to have her close by where I could see her.

It was a wintry morning, when I woke up and glanced over to her room as I usually did. But something didn't seem right. I ran over to her to find a strange phenomenon had occurred. The entire wall she was sleeping against had turned to a SHEET OF ICE! I'm talking about actual ice which formed on the inside of the wall. It didn't make sense. It was cold outside, but not that cold…and it was the only wall it happened to. We quickly woke her up and got her warm. But several days later she came down ill.

I tried calling the medical clinic to speak to Dr. Ron, our family practitioner, but I was told that he was on vacation. I didn't think I should wait for Cecilia to see someone, so I took her to a pediatrician a few blocks from our home. Both of our children had seen him in the past, and I felt he was a doctor I could trust. I made sure I told him about the strange incident of Cecilia's bedroom wall turning to ice a few days prior. He checked her over and said it appeared she just had a severe cold or possibly a virus. He prescribed some cough medicine and told us to give her acetaminophen for the fever. Then he turned to me and said, "Don't worry…she'll be fine."

When I got her home, I laid her on the couch. I noticed however, that she was shivering…most likely from the fever. I took her temperature and it wasn't extremely high, so I just gave her the acetaminophen the doctor recommended, and waited.

After a few minutes, a sudden panic came over me. "Something's wrong!" I said.

"What do you mean, Lisa?" Carlos replied, "The doctor said she was fine."

"I don't know!" I cried out, "I just know something's not right!"

I couldn't explain it. I just felt a certain dread come over me. Our baby girl was in trouble. I had Carlos scoop her up and get her ready to take her to the hospital as I reached for the phone to call Dr. Ron.

Over the years, we had grown close to him and he had given us his personal phone number just in case we ever needed it. I felt this was one of those times, and it proved to be a blessing we would not soon forget.

The phone rang for what seemed like an eternity and then finally his voice mail kicked in. As soon as it beeped, I talked a hundred miles an hour.

"Dr. Ron, this is Lisa Rodriguez. Please, I know you are on vacation, but if by any chance you are in town, we need you! Something is wrong with Cecilia. We are rushing her to St. Francis Hospital. If you can, please meet us there!"

Back then we only had the land line phones—no cell phones, so I knew there wasn't any way he could call us back. I just had to trust God would make sure Dr. Ron heard the message if he was meant to be there. After all, I was convinced this was the test the LORD had warned us about; so surely He would guide us now when we needed Him most.

We prayed fervently in the car crying out to God for help. As we were racing down the streets, it was as though the whole world slowed down. We were only a few minutes away from the hospital, but it seemed like we had been driving for hours. Finally we arrived and the doctor began to look Cecilia over.

Just as the emergency room doctor finished his examination, Dr. Ron came running in. "You came!" I said with tears in my eyes, "Oh thank you!" I took a deep breath as I realized that everything was working for our good. We informed Dr. Ron of the frozen wall, knowing it played an important role to what was happening to Cecilia. He immediately took over and began to ask the Emergency doctor what his assessment was. After checking her over himself, Dr. Ron requested Cecilia be admitted. That alone, I believe was a miracle. He had said her fever wasn't extremely high, but he just didn't feel comfortable releasing her. "I want to keep her at least overnight" Dr. Ron said, "It's just for precautionary measures."

I was relieved to hear him say those words. I knew in my heart we needed her somewhere safe. This one decision, I would find out later, saved her life.

Carlos and I were instructed to fill out the paperwork for her admittance while they took Cecilia to her room. We sat for quite a while before they called us to go to her. I knew hospitals were slow getting people situated in their rooms, so I didn't think much about it. But we would soon learn the delay was for more than just the typical reason.

I stayed with my daughter the entire night and Carlos went home with our infant. Cecilia had been placed on IV bags of antibiotics and solutions to keep her hydrated. The next morning the nurse came in.

"Oh, there's the little girl we saved last night!" she said.

"What?" I questioned—I was startled.

The nurse then proceeded to tell us the story. As Cecilia was being wheeled up to her room, the fever spiked to over 106 and she began to convulse. The nurse said they had to place her on a bed of ice and the situation turned critical. "We almost lost her!" the nurse said.

I thought Cecilia would only be there overnight, but for the next five days we were in that hospital with antibiotics and fluids running through her veins. I questioned my doctor on the third day, wanting clarity as to what we were fighting. He looked at me intently and spoke words which sent chills up my spine. "Lisa," he said intently, "we don't know what this is...but whatever it is, IT is trying to kill her!"

His words pierced my heart like an arrow. "It's trying to kill her?" I questioned in my heart. "What is?" I pondered.

Dr. Ron had taken blood work and urine samples, yet he was speaking of this thing as though it was a tangible, thinking personality. His statement frightened me. This was more than just an illness; this was a spiritual attack.

So, I asked him plainly. "Doctor, what would have happened if I just gave her the medicine like I was told to and didn't bring her in?"

"Lisa," he said shaking his head, "she would have convulsed in the night and died."

What words can you express to God in a moment like that? My mind traveled to the events which occurred. There was no outward evidence that day that she was in danger. And then there was the unexplainable incident at our home. How does an inside wall turn to a sheet of ice? It never happened before or after. It was a phenomenon we couldn't explain. To me, it was evident this was a spiritual assassin coming with the intent of killing our daughter. I didn't understand why, but in the end it didn't matter. What counted was our God WAS and IS a Deliverer, who promises: *"no weapon that is formed against you will prosper" (Isaiah 54:17 NASB).*

When I think of the "what if's" I realize how marvelous His works are.

- What if He hadn't given me the dream?
- What if I hadn't heeded it?
- What if I hadn't prepared for it through fasting and prayer?
- What if Dr. Ron wouldn't have given us his home phone number months earlier?
- What if he wouldn't have admitted her?

None of this was left to chance; the LORD took care of every detail assuring Cecilia's protection. This is enough to convince me that God cares deeply for what happens to His children and though we may go through some hard times, He *will not* allow *anything* to transpire that is not filtered first through His hands!

Let us always be alert when God speaks; for He sends us His message through many different avenues. It may be through the typical sermon or through Bible reading. Possibly, His message comes through prayers spoken at a prayer group or through a normal everyday conversation. For me, it was through a dream. But no matter how or when God speaks, we need to immediately obey. You just never know what it may cost you, if you don't.

He that dwelleth in the secret place of the most High shall abide under the shadow of the Almighty.
² I will say of the LORD, He is my refuge and my fortress: my God; in him will I trust.
³ Surely he shall deliver thee from the snare of the fowler, and from the noisome pestilence.
⁴ He shall cover thee with his feathers, and under his wings shalt thou trust: his truth shall be thy shield and buckler.
⁵ Thou shalt not be afraid for the terror by night; nor for the arrow that flieth by day;
⁶ Nor for the pestilence that walketh in darkness; nor for the destruction that wasteth at noonday.
⁷ A thousand shall fall at thy side, and ten thousand at thy right hand; but it shall not come nigh thee.
⁸ Only with thine eyes shalt thou behold and see the reward of the wicked.
⁹ Because thou hast made the LORD, which is my refuge, even the most High, thy habitation;
¹⁰ There shall no evil befall thee, neither shall any plague come nigh thy dwelling.
¹¹ For he shall give his angels charge over thee, to keep thee in all thy ways.
¹² They shall bear thee up in their hands, lest thou dash thy foot against a stone.
¹³ Thou shalt tread upon the lion and adder: the young lion and the dragon shalt thou trample under feet.
¹⁴ Because he hath set his love upon me, therefore will I deliver him: I will set him on high, because he hath known my name.
¹⁵ He shall call upon me, and I will answer him: I will be with him in trouble; I will deliver him, and honour him.
¹⁶ With long life will I satisfy him, and shew him my salvation.
Psalm 91 (KJV)

Think About It!

1.   Has the LORD ever given you a dream that came to pass?

2.   Was there ever a time the LORD warned you about impending danger for yourself or a loved one? What action did you take?

3.   Does it bring comfort to you to know God sees all things and nothing happens that isn't filtered through Him first?

4.   How important is it to *immediately* obey God? Was there ever a time you hesitated?

5.   What things can you do to help yourself become more aware when God is speaking to you?

Write About It!

Chapter Ten

If the Enemy is Under My Feet, Why is He Way Up There?

As the billowing winds echo with low mysterious tones, an eeriness sweeps across the land. Summer says goodbye as fall appears, announcing change is at the door. Change—a forceful rival to the present. It demands our attention as it signals a shift in our lives. At times, it can flood us with an adrenaline rush as we excitingly anticipate a transition to something good. But other times, it can leave us with that same eerie feeling as the change of seasons bring. Especially when the spiritual weather shifts to position us on the bottom…while the circumstances and trials are successfully on top!

In *1 Samuel 14*, we read about such a time for the Israelites, a shift in the season which fills them with anxiety and dread. The Philistines, we are told by historians, were successful in keeping iron weapons out of the hands of the Hebrews. In Nelson's *New Illustrated* Bible Manners &

Customs (page 189), it is said only King Saul and Jonathan had the proper weapons and body armor, while the rest were left to fight with inferior ones: clubs, bows and slings. Now the Philistines managed to encamp high upon a cliff, while the Israelites were positioned in the valley below. To top it off, there were only 600 soldiers with King Saul, leaving them at a great disadvantage.

You would think Saul, being the King of Israel, would be off somewhere seeking the face of God, offering Him sacrifices and pleading for help. But instead we find him sitting under a pomegranate tree. This was just another visual reminder of his poor leadership and lack of devotion to God. King Saul over the years had sadly forgotten, *"The Lord's eyes keep on roaming throughout the earth, looking for those whose hearts completely belong to him, so that he may strongly support them…" (2Chronicles 16:9 ISV)*.

God reveals His desire to help people if they will give Him their whole heart, but King Saul proves over and over again through his actions that he is only *partially* devoted to God, and then, only if it benefits himself.

But there was one in the camp who remembered God's goodness and trusted him completely; it was King Saul's son, Jonathan. *1Samuel 14:6 (NIV)* states *"Jonathan said to his young armor bearer, "Come, let's go over to the outpost of those uncircumcised men. Perhaps the LORD will act in our behalf. Nothing can hinder the LORD from saving, whether by many or by few."*

Did he say by few? He wasn't kidding! There were only two against a multitude, Jonathan and his armor bearer. Now that's faith! While his father chose to cowardly sit under a tree, Jonathan took his armor bearer and went after the Philistines, refusing to remain on the bottom.

There is a clue to Jonathan's amazing bravery, a clue which can help us when our battles seem insurmountable. It is found in Jonathan's words, *"Come, let's go over to the outpost of those uncircumcised men."*

You see, Jonathan was banking on the fact that the Philistines were not circumcised; a very important detail. Circumcision was a sign of the covenant promised to the Israelites by God. It was a binding agreement, sealed within their flesh; a constant reminder the LORD would be with them in every life situation. The Philistines did not have this covenant, nor feared God; therefore, they were not under His protection.

For this reason, in Jonathan's eyes of faith, it was not the Israelites who were at a disadvantage, but rather the Philistines.

It is not easy to have this kind of faith we see in Jonathan, especially when we find ourselves on the bottom, trapped by situations beyond our control. I believe we have all faced trials at one time or another, which were so overwhelming it seemed like we were suffocating under the weight of its pressure. But it is in those moments we need to remember, like Jonathan, *"…If God is for us, who can be against us" (Romans 8:31 NIV)?* It is clear that God's promises are "Yes and Amen." It's settled. The end. Period. No discussion, no maybes. If God has promised He will be on our side and will not abandon us, it is enough.

This revelation of trusting in our Heavenly Father, who promised to have our back, should help all of us in our time of need; to bring the courage and faith to fight no matter the odds! The Lord is looking for a dauntless trust in Him…and He will reward it with His delivering power. Jonathan had complete confidence in the LORD, even though the fight seemed impossible, and because he believed, God shifted their position from the bottom to the top!

Jonathan's heroic faith was a huge contrast to his father. While Jonathan acted out his faith, fervently climbing with hands and feet up the jagged rocks of the cliff, his father arose from under the tree and attempted to give a "show" of faith. It was King Saul's hope that he could fool God into responding to his religious acts as he put on a display of sacrificing unto the LORD. But our Heavenly Father, searches man's heart and is a *"discerner of the thoughts and intents" (Hebrews 4:12 KJV)*. King Saul was wicked; and the Lord had already in His wisdom rejected him. Even the prophet Samuel was no longer with him, forcing King Saul to bring another prophet to worship unto God. But just as the sacrifice was in motion, something begins to happen within the Philistine camp. God rises up to meet Jonathan's advances proving He will be there in the time of trouble for those who are devoted to Him!

Jonathan and his armor bearer kill approximately 20 of the Philistines when God steps in and takes over. Because faith is revealed by action, God is able to use Jonathan and his armor bearer's aggressive acts to stir the Philistines into a frenzy of confusion. The Philistines in the hectic commotion, begin to turn on each other! When King Saul realizes there is something happening, he immediately stops the prophet who was ready to sacrifice unto God. King Saul couldn't even wait to worship, but rather runs off to pursue the battle against the Philistines. Once again, King Saul reveals his false devotion is nothing more than a tool to get what he wants.

Where is your heart when it appears the enemy is on top? Sometimes trials are used by God to test where our heart is. *Proverbs 17:3* (NASB) states, *"The refining pot is for silver and the furnace for gold, But the Lord tests the hearts."*

This story reveals two hearts, two options. When you find yourself in a battle where the circumstances are outside your reach, it is then you will have to make a choice. You can fearfully hide like King Saul and cry wimpy, faithless prayers, or you can arise like Jonathan, boldly declaring God will deliver.

We have a powerful, risen Savior and He will surely be with us in our time of need. Like Jonathan, we can bank on it! So when we find the enemy on top when he should be under our feet, remember throughout the scriptures there is a promise to all of us—God's chosen people:

Be strong and of good courage, do not fear nor be afraid of them; for the Lord your God, He is the One who goes with you. He will not leave you nor forsake you."
(Deuteronomy 31:6 KJV)

Think About It

1. Have you ever sensed a change of season was coming into your life? Were you excited or fearful?

2. Did you ever experience a time, where against all odds, God came through for you?

3. Did you ever cowardly hide from a hard trial? Was there a time when you arose in faith? What was the outcome of those trials?

4. Did you ever sense God using trials to test where your heart was? What did those trials reveal?

Write About It

Chapter Eleven

When Life is Stuck in Pause

It was one of those late Friday afternoons, when "be lazy" was on the list of things to do. It wasn't often I could just relax. There on the couch, with remote in hand, I was enjoying my family as we watched an old time movie. Without warning, the doorbell rang, not once, but several times in succession. It was as though that bell was voicing an opinion, "Open quickly now!"

My husband hurried to the door as I lagged behind. I just couldn't seem to get myself going. Yet I was curious as to who was at my door! While I made my way over, my husband unlocked the latch. The door flung open, as though from a forceful wind, and I watched as my oldest daughter Ceci, collapsed into my husband's arms. "Papa, the baby is gone!" she sobbed. I stood frozen as her piercing cries flung like arrows into my heart.

"How could this be possible?" I thought. Only two weeks prior, she was joyfully talking about the baby bouncing around in her womb.

Surely there must be a mistake! In one moment of a door ring, our relaxing movie night turned dark and a downpour of a storm hovered over us. "This isn't real." I told myself. "Can we change this channel?" I wondered, "Who hit the pause button and left us standing in the rain?"

Ceci and her husband, Dan, started to go over the details of their day. They said they had a regular baby appointment, just a check-up. But that appointment turned into a dreaded nightmare. As the doctor went about her routine, a sudden concern came upon her face. There was no heartbeat. Dead silence in a womb where only weeks before was alive with the sounds of their second child. With frantic hearts, they had two ultrasounds that day, and it was confirmed that the baby was no longer alive.

The sounds that filled our living room only moments ago, had dissipated into the air as we all stood in complete silence. "Was I breathing?" I wondered. I wasn't sure. I felt as though my chest was tightening around me, squeezing out every bit of breath I had. My mind began racing for a solution…but none came. A hurricane had blown into our home, and with it the dread of having no control over the tragic events that were happening.

Reaching for hope, I looked at my daughter and said, "We don't need to accept this!

This doesn't feel right. Let's pray for God to turn it around." Ceci's eyes suddenly lit up with encouragement. In all the commotion, she forgot the prognosis was not final—God still had the last say.

It was two agonizing weeks before her next appointment and we prayed fervently, hoping for a miracle. I was at work when she called. My heart was crushed as she spoke, "Nothing has changed, but it is ok Mama. We are going to keep on believing!" The prognosis was exactly the same; the baby was gone.

I was so proud of my daughter and the stand of faith she was taking. Yet I found myself overwhelmed by the thought of her going through this horrible ordeal. I put my head down on the desk and sobbed.

Dan had a scheduled youth conference that weekend and was going to cancel to stay with Ceci. However, she didn't want him to. She felt that he could do nothing for her by staying, but he could win souls and minister to the youth if he went. He was reluctant to go, but she insisted.

"Kick the devil *real good* for me!" she said, "I will stay with my folks. Don't worry, it will be fine." My daughter and I stayed in the master bedroom that night. She was spot bleeding, but we just kept speaking the blessings of God. We sang…we prayed…we cried…and we stretched our hands to heaven hoping to grasp a miracle.

As we talked, Ceci confided in me that for months she was dying spiritually and had been asking God to awaken her once again. It was clear to her now that she would have lost her mind had she just accepted this bad report without question. She needed these two weeks of prayer to change the empty well of her heart, to face whatever may come. Exhausted by the intensity of the hour, we finally fell asleep.

Several hours later, Ceci woke up and felt like she couldn't breathe. I got her into the car and began to drive to the hospital. But when we drew near, she had me pull into a Walgreens parking lot instead. Her labored breathing appeared to be more from anxiety than anything else; and it was clear she wasn't yet ready to give up.

"Let's go home." Ceci said. I asked her if she was sure that is what she wanted to do. "Yes." She said emphatically.

I drove back home and upon entering the bedroom, we both fell exhausted upon the bed. Completely spent, we fell into a deep sleep.

As the dawn broke, I saw Ceci get out of bed and walk to the middle of the room. It was there she lay prostrate on the floor for some time praying. In her brokenness she whispered, "I surrender Lord. No matter what, I will praise you!" She then stood up and her water immediately broke.

I drove her to the hospital, trying to hide my despair. Clearly God wasn't intervening as we had hoped. I became frightened that I would lose my faith forever, never to trust God again. How could we possibly recover from this?

Ceci was rushed to a cold, clinical room. The walls were grey, appropriate for the bleak cloud that covered us. As she lay on the bed, the nurses tried frantically to slow down the bleeding. Turning her head towards me, my daughter cried out, "Mommy! I don't want to do this!"

"I know." I said softly as I stroked her head, "I know baby. It will be okay."

A pan was used to collect the blood. At one point, I saw the nurses look down into the pan and then look sadly at each other. I knew what was happening. The baby had passed.

Oh how I wanted to fix this! There was my little girl, with tears rolling down her face like she had so many years ago when she bumped her toe and scraped her knee. I was able to dry those tears…these I could not.

I bent down to put my face close to hers. Courage began to rise up within me as I determined to walk her through this strenuous time. But suddenly there was another presence, tangible and strong. An incredible peace rushed into the room and between me and my daughter; Jesus was there! His presence said, "Peace be still, I AM HERE." And He was.

A special surgical team was called in—Ceci had lost a lot of blood and they had to stop it. As they wheeled her away, I could tell she thought she would die. "You're not going anywhere!" I said.

I prayed fervently while she was being worked on and believed the LORD to keep her in His care. Ceci had too much destiny in her to be taken now…I knew that. From the time she was in my womb, He had great plans for her. She would fulfill them.

The next few months obviously were very difficult, but our faith was intact! Just knowing that the LORD was there in that room comforted me and I was believing our Heavenly Father would slowly heal my daughter's heart.

Over a year later, Ceci went on to have a baby boy and is now pregnant with her third child. She is an incredible mom and wife. She also teaches Christian dance and choreographs much of our church musicals. She is a singer, dancer, teacher…and she does it all for the Glory of God! The devil may have had a plan for the destruction of Ceci's faith, hoping to destroy her ability to go on when she went through this miscarriage. But just the opposite happened. Ceci and the family became stronger, and our faith and trust in God increased!

A valuable lesson was learned through all of this heartache, which would be forever embedded in our hearts. When the storms hit and life is stuck in pause, the outcome—good or bad—is never as powerful as the revelation of knowing God will always, without fail, be there.

> *"The Lord is close to the brokenhearted and saves those who are crushed in spirit."*
> *(Psalm 34:18 NASB)*

Think About It!

1. Do you remember a time when you were enjoying the day and suddenly bad news came?

2. Describe how you feel when troubles come that are outside of your control?

3. Was there ever a time you were afraid you would lose your faith? What did you do to build it up?

4. In everyone's life there will be times of sunshine, as well as stormy rain clouds. Yet, God promises that He will never leave us. Has there ever been a difficult moment in your life when God rushed in and revealed His presence to you?

Write About It!

Chapter Twelve

The Sweet Fragrance of God

The moment I anointed my head with oil, the Lord's presence flooded my room like a rushing waterfall. My nostrils were filled with the wonderful scent of frankincense and myrrh, a fragrance I had grown to love. I often sensed my Heavenly Papa when using this particular oil. I had grown accustomed to it; much like my children who knew when their father was close by, due to his scented cologne filling the air.

My prayer time had become sweet, unlike anything I had experienced before. I was surprisingly energized as new revelations unfolded before me in the Word of God. So close was the Lord to me, I think I wouldn't have been able to get any closer this side of heaven!

It wasn't always that way with me. I use to be quite distant from God, even as a Christian. Many years ago as a new believer, I didn't know what a "Heavenly Father" was. So I began associating Him with what I *perceived* natural fathers to be. It was a tainted viewpoint.

Most of the Fathers I knew growing up, including my own, just wanted to see their children doing their best. However, somewhere along the way, I translated their good intentions to mean children had to WIN their father's approval. This sent me on a road demanding I do my utmost ALL the time; I had become a hopeless perfectionist. Of course, with such an attitude, you never quite meet the standard you set for yourself. In my eyes…not my father's…I was never good enough.

Unfortunately, I carried this viewpoint into my relationship with God. If I prayed one hour, I was beating myself over the head for not praying two. If I read a chapter of the Bible before bed, I questioned why I didn't read at least three or four. I was in constant fear of being rejected by the LORD and became a slave to the taskmaster of religion. In my estimation, I never quite measured up to what I thought God expected of me. I was constantly begging the Lord for forgiveness for falling short and made promises to do better. My salvation became a work of trying to obtain God's approval in the hopes of one day pleasing Him.

I thank God for *Ephesians 2:8-9 (HCSB)* that states, *"For you are saved by grace through faith, and this is not from yourselves; it is God's gift—not from works, so that no one can boast."*

It took me two long years of my Christian life before I got this scripture embedded within my soul; and it took God's intervention to make it happen. While in my bedroom praying one day, I had a glorious vision of our Savior. The heavens opened up before me, right in my room, and there was Jesus looking down from the cross. His eyes pierced my entire being with a love so indescribable, I would not dare explain it with human words. I had been taught Christ loved all of us so much, He died in our place. But somehow, I could never comprehend it until I saw that vision in my room. Then I understood! His sacrifice was enough.

As His love poured into the depths of my soul, it was made quite clear…never was my performance the reason I was accepted by the Heavenly Father, but rather because of the blood sacrifice of His Son. Prior to this vision, I thought the fear of the LORD meant I should tremble and tread lightly before a God who was ready to pounce on any mistake I made! Now He was allowing me to see not His judgment, but a great love displayed in His sacrifice for me. Jesus gave His very life because He *valued* who I was, with all my attributes and shortcomings.

This vision forever changed my mindset. I can say most emphatically, "I am the Shepherd's daughter! I don't have to win His love—I already have it. I don't do right because I am afraid of God; I do what is right because I love God. He has put His nature in me so that my spirit longs to be like Him. The fear I now hold for the LORD is a "reverence" and "awe," not a fear of judgment. How could I be afraid of my Papa? His blood runs through my veins.

This understanding brings a breath-taking realization that there are benefits to being His child. We will sometimes soar successfully to the highest of heights; and at other times fall flat on our face! Yet no matter the outcome, The Heavenly Father's love remains constant for us, and He is always on our side to establish victory.

There is another benefit which may not initially appear to be good. It's the benefit of God, as our Father, taking on the responsibility of having to discipline us when we need it… a thought which isn't very palatable when you are on the receiving end!

Hebrews 12:11 in the Living Bible says it marvelously:

"Being punished isn't enjoyable while it is happening—it hurts! But afterwards we can see the result, a quiet growth in grace and character."

Our Heavenly Father will correct us when He has to. Some may look at this as a God ready to slam His gavel down upon us with severity. But it is His love, not judgment that disciplines us, and it is a great benefit in keeping us safe. If, for example, a parent sees a child getting ready to dash out into the street after being told numerous times not to do such a thing, would you think bad of them for giving that child a spanking? Not at all. The parent wants the child to know how serious of an act it is. If the child *remembers* that spanking next time he or she gets an urge to go into the street, it will keep that child from stepping out into danger. Good parents are willing to cause temporary pain to save their child from unnecessary suffering.

"Young man, do not resent it when God chastens and corrects you, for his punishment is proof of his love. Just as a father punishes a son he delights in to make him better, so the Lord corrects you" Proverbs 3:12 (TLB).

God's heart for us is pure love. It encompasses all that a Father is to His beloved children—teacher, disciplinary, encourager, counselor, protector…the list goes on. Yet I have found over the years, multiple Christians who struggle with the idea of God loving them unconditionally, as a good and righteous Father! Sadly, if we don't allow God to pierce the depths of our soul with this revelation of a Heavenly Father's love, we may find ourselves among those who are constantly tossed between the freedom of the cross and the bondage of religion.

Religion is the opposite of God's plan. It demands perfectionism, self-righteousness and a high standard outside of man's reach. Why live in a place of religious condemnation when you can enjoy the fullness of God's love…paid by the price of His Son?

The promise found in *James 4:8* is simple: if we will draw near to Him, He will draw near to us. The most magnificent truth of the Father-Creator interacting with His creation is this: He will personally fellowship with each one of us according to our personality and character! He created each of His children differently; none of us are exactly the same.

And because of this, He will draw you into a relationship where the sweet fragrance of God is unique and personal…made special for you!

All those led by God's Spirit are God's sons. For you did not receive a spirit of slavery to fall back into fear, but you received the Spirit of adoption, by whom we cry out, "Abba, Father!" The Spirit Himself testifies together with our spirit that we are God's children, and if children, also heirs—heirs of God and coheirs with Christ—seeing that we suffer with Him so that we may also be glorified with Him.
(Romans 8:14-18 HCSB)

But thanks be to God! For through what Christ has done, he has triumphed over us so that now wherever we go he uses us to tell others about the Lord and to spread the Gospel like a sweet perfume. [15] As far as God is concerned there is a sweet, wholesome fragrance in our lives. It is the fragrance of Christ within us, an aroma to both the saved and the unsaved all around us.
(2Corinthians 2:14-15 TLB)

Think About It!

1.   What did you think the first time you heard that God was your Heavenly Father? Did it help you to relate more to Him; or did it cause more of a disconnection?

2.   Have there been times in your Christian walk where you struggled with perfectionism or felt like you just didn't measure up?

3.   Where do you go to spend time alone with the LORD?

4.   Share a time when God came to you in a sweet way.

Write About It!

Chapter Thirteen

Waves

The water clapped like thunder as it rolled over my head. Struggling to stay above the rhythmic motion of the waves, I thought to myself, "This is what it is like to drown." Gasping for air, I kept swallowing what seemed like gallons of water as I frantically tried to swim to safety. Every time my head broke through the water, I would try and take a breath, but the waves continued to engulf me, forcing more water down my throat.

Finally after what seemed like an eternity, someone noticed I was in trouble. I wasn't drowning in the middle of a salty ocean, nor a violent sea. Neither was I plunging helplessly down a raging river. No…this talented lady was gracefully drowning in the crowded, wave pool at a theme park in Wisconsin Dells! The lifeguard casually looked down at me as I continued to gulp in water and said, "Are you o.k.?" I stupidly nodded, "Yes."

It seems inconceivable to me, that I chose such a critical time to be prideful! I ashamedly didn't want her to know I couldn't handle the waves little children were splashing in; so I basically was allowing myself to drown! Luckily for me, the lifeguard ignored my foolishness and extended her flotation device towards me as I went under one more time. Grabbing the device, I hung on for dear life as she pulled me towards the shallow waters. I tried to give her my thanks, but I could barely breathe, and my throat literally burned from all the water. I just gave her a forced grin and waved to her as I left the pool. From this experience I determined waves can be dangerous!

I guess that's why when I read the story of *Matthew 14:22-33*, I don't blame the disciples for being frightened. After feeding a crowd of over 5,000, Jesus sends his apostles off in a boat while he withdraws to a secluded place to pray. The Bible states the boat was already quite a distance from land and was being battered by the waves. It grew dark and foreboding. Can you imagine what they must have felt like?

The blackness of the night was like a blanket over the sea and Jesus was not with them to provide them with the comfort and peace they needed. Not being able to see what may be lurking in those waters, the eerie wind pierces through with frightening noises. Trapped in the middle of the sea, they sense their vulnerability as the threat of violent waves attempt to capsize their boat. Suddenly, off in the darkness a shadow appears. It is a horrible sight! An apparition walking on the water approaches them as they sit there like prey in the night. It was a nightmare out of a horror story, but they were actually living it.

Frozen with fear, they scream out, "It's a ghost!" Luckily for them, it actually was Jesus, supernaturally walking on the water towards them. I can only imagine their relief as Jesus speaks, "Have courage! It is I. Don't be afraid."

You would think this would be the end of the story: the disciples get in trouble and Jesus saves them. *The End.* But it wasn't the end at all. In fact, Peter makes an astonishing request.

"Lord, if it's You," Peter answered Him, *"command me to come to You on the water."*

"Come!" He said (Matthew 14:28 HCSB).

What compelled Peter after such a horrible night to take a risk and get out onto those waters? I can tell you most Christians would say Peter wanted to experience something supernatural. After all, don't we all? But I can tell you, that is not the case in this story. Peter **was already** experiencing supernatural events as he walked with Jesus. So then…what was it? Peter's words reveal his true heart's motivation. He didn't ask for power to walk on water or authority to rebuke the waves. He wasn't seeking to do something cool or supernatural. He just wanted to come…come to where Jesus was.

Because of Peter's longing and deep desire to be where his Savior was—the supernatural came. It's an important thought that the Church World has forgotten.

I see every day, thousands of Christians flocking to any hint of revival they can find. Desiring "a touch of the Spirit," they run from one place to another in the hopes of a supernatural move. But that mentality doesn't strengthen our relationship with the LORD. In fact, it can move us from a personal, discipleship-type relationship with Christ to a more distant one; much like the casual multitudes which followed Jesus only for His works.

Wanting only the food Jesus produced supernaturally, much of the crowd, who were fed miraculously with five loaves and two fishes, boarded boats to find Jesus in Capernaum. You would think if the crowd was willing to travel so far, they must have desired the deeper revelations Jesus taught. But Jesus knew otherwise. He tells them, *"I assure you: You are looking for Me, not because you saw the signs, but because you ate the loaves and were filled. Don't work for the food that perishes but for the food that lasts for eternal life, which the Son of Man will give you, because God the Father has set His seal of approval on Him" (John 6:26-27 HCSB).*

As Jesus began to reveal He was the bread of life, they started to complain, taking offense in who He claimed to be. This crowd was not at all interested in the secret things of God. Instead their response was just the opposite. Just feed us. Make us feel good. Bless us. But don't get too deep. Don't try to say we must have this personal relationship with you!

Jesus is radical in His ways and doesn't care about their offenses. He takes this conversation over the top by shocking them with His next words: they had to eat His flesh and drink His blood in order to have eternal life! As strange as this comment may have been to them, this was a revelation which could have changed their lives forever if they were willing to search it out. But instead, they chose to stop following Jesus. They literally turned away! It was just way too hard for their fleshly minds to comprehend.

The crowds sought extraordinary workings which would only satisfy their flesh. Honestly, when we jump from revival to revival seeking only the supernatural manifestations, we are no better than the crowds of Jesus' day. We are basically saying the same things: Just feed us. Make us feel good. Bless us. We want the thrills, the goose bumps, the oohs and aahs of the Spirit. But don't make us work for anything. Don't tell us that we have to go deeper.

Think about it. The Bible doesn't say, "Go out into the next revival and these signs shall follow." No, it says, *"Go out into all the world and preach the gospel…and these signs will follow those who believe…" (Mark 16:15-17 NKJV)*.

Peter had it right. His desire to walk on water was not for power, but so he could simply draw closer to the LORD. It was during his pursuit of Jesus, even in the midst of a windy storm that caused him to step out into the supernatural. And though Jesus had to help him, he was learning how to trust God and walk where no other men dared to go. In the end, Peter was among the greatest apostles of his time and went on to perform many miracles in Jesus's name.

The Supernatural Power of God is found in our relationship with Christ and our obedience to Him. Jesus said, *"Don't work for the food that perishes but for the food that lasts for eternal life…" (John 6:27 HCSB)*.

Eating His flesh and drinking His blood was speaking of the covenant of eternal life which He invites each one of us to partake in. It was an invitation to come in deeper…to know

Him intimately, and to learn to walk in the life-giving flow of His Spirit.

Don't get me wrong; revivals have their place. But it is not to *replace* our intimacy with God. We don't chase revivals—instead we chase the LORD! We also obey His command to go out and preach the gospel. It is then, that the supernatural follows. The power in the church has been lost because we have not obeyed the command to GO! We simply want to STAY and enjoy the benefits of God, while the world drowns in a pool of sin and despair.

There are many turbulent waves covering the lives of people—people we are to lead to Christ. At times, they may need us to extend to them a spiritual flotation device and pull them to safety. Other times, they may need for us to take their hand and walk with them as they attempt to rise above the turbulent circumstances of their lives.

As God's people, let us not look for supernatural events which are here tomorrow and gone the next day. Rather, let's inhale the grace of the LORD that is available. Let's breathe His presence so deeply that when we exhale... the faith of God will manifest in miraculous ways, saving those around us! We can learn to walk on water every day if we penetrate the depths of the Holy Spirit and allow Him to lead and guide us into the Truth and Righteousness of the LORD. For only in this kind of life can we truly ride the waves…and teach others to do so as well.

> *Mightier than the thunder of the great waters,*
> *mightier than the breakers of the sea—*
> *the LORD on high is mighty*
> *(Psalms 93:4 NIV)*

Think About It!

1. Was there ever a time you took a risk and stepped out in the LORD only to become frightened?

2. Have you ever been used by God in a supernatural way?

3. Be honest and look back over your life. Was there ever a time when seeking supernatural manifestations of the Spirit, took precedence over seeking God?

4. Has the LORD ever spoken something to you that was too hard for you to understand? Were you tempted to walk away like the crowd who heard Jesus say they must eat His flesh…or did you seek the LORD more earnestly until that revelation was revealed?

Write About It!

Chapter Fourteen

The Book of Remembrance

Soaring upon the written pages of this book, the Spirit of God ascends like a gentle dove upon the memories of the past. His Grace is evidently present in every area of our lives: during times of sadness and laughter, successes and failures, faith and courage…even moments of a little silliness and humor. These events in our lives are all carefully handled by the Master's hands and meticulously woven into a beautiful tapestry—for all the world to see.

This is a book of remembrance. A book that proves without a shadow of a doubt, we serve a living God. A God who interacts, intervenes and literally breathes upon our lives in the most astonishing ways. His love is endless, gliding over the years of our life like a grand ship upon the waves of the sea. It guides us through days of sunshine and nights of storms to the port of our final destination…our Heavenly Home.

While doing my devotionals one day, I read this scripture:

*"Then those who feared and loved the Lord spoke often of him to each other. And he had a **Book of Remembrance** drawn up in which he recorded the names of those who feared him and loved to think about him"* (Malachi 3:16 TLB).

As I finished this scripture, the LORD whispered, "This book you are writing is *your* book of remembrance!"

You see, each chapter of "Oxygenate" reveals the joys and struggles of life. It takes you on a journey with me through ordinary Christianity that allows us to be "real!" Admit it—isn't it wonderful to be able to exhale a deep sigh of relief and say, "it's okay to be me?" Honesty flows out as you freely acknowledge your greatest successes and deepest failures; understanding that both are used by God to help mold you into more of His image.

It wasn't until the last chapter was written that I realized how significant this was. You see, He orchestrated the pages of this book in ways I didn't quite understand. A "Write About It" page was placed after each chapter. It was His will—His design. It was intended for journaling your own story of how the Heavenly Father moved in your life during similar circumstances. But it wasn't until I was almost finished, that the LORD spoke something remarkable to me, revealing His ultimate plan for that page. God said, "Tell them…go back."

Go back to the "Write About It" pages. Copy each one and then staple them together. The Heavenly Father says this is now *YOUR* glorious story…your personal book of remembrance. A testimony of God's grace for all to see!

My prayer is that you will begin to read over your little book and clearly observe how God has oxygenated every part of your life. Among the pages, may you recognize a growth and courage you had not pondered before. I pray His Majestic Love becomes so evident in your story that you will come to the conclusion that in the cycle of inhaling grace and exhaling faith—the simplicity of life radiates with God's wonder.

If you didn't complete the "Write About It" pages—no worries, there's still time. Go back. Read the stories and then write yours with the knowledge that an Amazing God was there with you…every step of the way. And until we have arrived safely to the port of our Heavenly Home…keep breathing my friends. We are almost there!

Oxygenate: Inhale Grace--Exhale Faith
Just Breathe!

Do You Know Him?

I hope you enjoyed your journey through the pages of "Oxygenate." It is my prayer that as you followed through each story and lesson, your faith was strengthened with the knowledge that God's grace is constant, His love unending.

Perhaps while reading, you pondered whether you could actually know God in such an intimate way as what was written. Maybe this was the first time you ever heard that God desires a relationship with you. Or perhaps you once were close to Him, but drifted away.

If so, I would like to give you an opportunity to pray to Jesus and ask Him to come in…into your life, your world, your heart. You don't have to be perfect for Him to accept you—in fact, that will never happen. God sent His Son, Jesus, to come to this earth and do what we could not: live a sinless life. And because of His perfection, because He died in our place and resurrected, we can receive life eternal if we will accept Him into our hearts. He simply says, "Come."

So let the failures, shortcomings and past mistakes of your life be removed by a God who makes all things new.

Open your heart wide and make the following prayer your own:

"God, I come to you now in the name of your son, Jesus. I recognize that I have lived my life in my own way, and consequently have left you out.

Take my life…I receive you as my God, my LORD, my Savior. Jesus, I believe that you came to this earth to pay the penalty for my sins. You died in my place so that I could have eternal life and I receive your gift now with joy.

How could I ever repay you? I can't. So I give you only what I can—I give you **me**; as I understand *all of me* is really all you want anyway. Take all that I am and all that I hope to be. From this day forward, teach me to inhale your incredible grace in every moment of my life and in turn exhale faith that changes the world around me. Amen."

If you have prayed this prayer with a sincere heart, then let me welcome you into the family of God and encourage you to tell someone you trust. Also, find a Bible-believing church that will help guide you on this new journey with Jesus!

There have been diligent and faithful people, who have joined together to make this book a possibility. If you have made a decision to follow Jesus, we would love to hear from you. Drop us an email at **inhalegrace@gmail.com** and let us know you have decided to follow the LORD.

May the Lord richly bless you, and may you feel His presence as you walk through this new way of life!

Made in the USA
Lexington, KY
28 January 2015